20 REASONS Why This Present Earth May Not Last Another 20 YEARS

by

SALEM KIRBAN

D0107227

First Printing ....February, 1973
Second Printing ....April, 1973
Third Printing ....December, 1973
Fourth Printing ....November, 1974

RIVERSIDE BOOK and BIBLE HOUSE
P.O. Box 904
Iowa Falls, Iowa 50126

ISBN 0-912582-07-3
Library of Congress Catalog Card No. 72-78026

WHY I WROTE THIS BOOK...

This was a difficult book to write. Yet it had to be written!

It required sifting through thousands of daily, weekly and monthly publications from all over the world...carefully culling out those news articles which had particular significance to the future of this present earth.

The title of this book may or may not be prophetic. 20 REASONS WHY THIS PRESENT EARTH MAY NOT LAST ANOTHER 20 YEARS...is a long and rather awesome title...frightening.

Notice the key word in the title is the word "MAY." This present earth *may not* last another 20 years. Then on the other hand, it *may* last more than 20 years. Only God knows.

It is important for us to realize that we are moving far more rapidly in every direction than we did even 100 years ago. Before World War 1, the lag between idea and use was 33 years. After World War 2, development time was down to 9 years. Now...from idea to use...development time is under 5 years. Then too, we have experienced a revolution in technology. One result has been that about 90% of all the scientists ever born are now living in this present era.

I am no prophet...nor am I a "sensationalist." Nor do I believe in burying my head in the sand. I am primarily a news analyst...scrutinizing every bit of news through the magnifying glass of Bible prophecy.

And what I see, in one sense, frightens me. The present earth system is coming to the point of no return. The time of the Rapture (when Christians will suddenly be caught up to be with Christ) is rapidly approaching. The world will soon be at the doorstep of Armageddon. Yet, as the Pharisees in Matthew 16...,many of us cannot discern the "...signs of the times...."

That's why I wrote this book!

Salem Kirban
Huntingdon Valley, Pennsylvania
January, 1973

4

CONTENTS

Why I Wrote This Book 4

Explanation of Terms Used in This Book 6

1 Population Perils 8

2 Earth's Limits 14

3 Water, The Vanishing Oasis 24

4 Taxing Taxes 32

5 Pregnancy by Permit 38

6 Food and Famine 44

7 Lovers of Pleasure 50

8 Bigger Barns 56

9 Israel's Return 64

10 Education's Demise 84

11 Mind Control 90

12 Moral Decay 94

13 The Church Conglomerate 98

14 Russia's Rise 104

15 Un-United States 114

16 The Forces of Antichrist Emerging 126

17 Common Market 138

18 Asia's Alliances 144

19 The X-Ray Sky 160

20 Armageddon's Arsenal 168

What Will You Do with Jesus 186

ACKNOWLEDGMENTS

To **Dr. Gary G. Cohen,** Professor of Greek and New Testament at Biblical School of Theology, Hatfield, Pa., who carefully checked the final manuscript.

To **Robert Krauss,** artist, who skillfully designed the front cover.

To **Doreen Frick,** who devoted many hours to proofreading the text.

To **Batsch Company,** for excellent craftsmanship in setting the type.

To **Walter W. Slotilock,** Chapel Hill Litho for making many of the negatives necessary for offset printing.

To **Dickinson Brothers, Inc.,** for producing under complex circumstances, an excellent printing of my book.

To the many **PHOTOGRAPHERS** throughout the world who pooled their resources so that we might have exclusive photographs that accurately depict these Last Days including Wide World Photos, Helmut K. Wimmer, Black Star, Magnum, NASA, New York Times, Compix, Bettman Archive, LIFE, Nancy Palmer Agency and Gamma.

Abomination of Desolation

A desecration of the temple by Antichrist. His final attempt to force the Jews to worship him (Matthew 24:15; II Thessalonians 2:3,4; Daniel 9:27).

Antichrist

A name taken from I and II John. In Daniel he is referred to as the little horn and the vile person; In II Thessalonians as the Son of Perdition; and in Revelation as the Beast out of the sea.

Satan so completely possesses the man as to amount almost to an incarnation. Scriptures appear to indicate that he, like Judas Iscariot, will become indwelt by Satan.

Antichrist will oppose Christ, the saints, and the Jews. He will be first hailed as a Man of Peace and given unlimited power by the European countries, the United States and Israel. At his rise, Antichrist will be only a man, but with satanic power. His sudden, sensational rise as the saviour of a world threatened by destruction will be one of the marks of the beginning of the Time of the End.

His later attempt to annihilate the Jews will bring about his defeat at Jerusalem by the return of Christ. All prophecy up to the return of Christ at Armegeddon will be fulfilled by the close of his day.

The False Prophet

Antichrist will be the political ruler who will work the works of Satan. **The False Prophet** will be the religious ruler who will undergird the work of the **Antichrist.** Both get their power from Satan.

The False Prophet never will attempt to promote himself. He will never become an object of worship. He will do the work of a prophet in that he directs attention away from himself to one who he says has the right to be worshipped (the Antichrist).

The False Prophet will imitate many miracles of God. He will cause fire to come down from heaven copying the miracles of Elijah in order to convince the nation Israel that he (The False Prophet) is the Elijah whom Malachi promised was yet to come (Malachi 4:5-6)! Having achieved this deception the False Prophet will declare that since this miracle (bringing fire from heaven) shows that he is Elijah...then, therefore, the Antichrist is truly Christ and should be worshipped.

He will also build a statue, and through some satanic miracle cause this statue (image) to talk and somehow come to life. When the people see this miracle they will fall down and worship the Antichrist believing him to be a Christ.

Last Days

Our reference to the Last Days means the *days immediately* prior to the "Rapture" of the saints and the ushering in of the Tribulation Period of 7 years.

Mark of the Beast

During the second half of the seven year Tribulation Period, the Antichrist (who previously was setting himself up as a Man of Peace) will suddenly move against the Jews and all those who have accepted Christ as Saviour during the first 3½ years of this Period. In Revelation 13:16,17 we read that "...he (False Prophet) causeth all, both small and great, rich and poor, free and bond, to receive some mark in their right hand, or in their foreheads: And that no man might buy or sell, save he that had the mark . . . "

Therefore those who refuse to submit to the authority of this system by having this mark (the Mark of the Beast), either starve to death slowly, or else are slain by the representatives of the government, who will treat as traitors all who refuse to accept this identifying mark.

Rapture

This refers to the time, prior to the start of the 7 year Tribulation Period, when believing Christians (both dead and alive) will "in the twinkling of an eye" rise up to meet Christ in the air.

"For the Lord himself shall descend from Heaven with a shout... and the dead in Christ shall rise first: Then we which are alive and remain shall be caught up (RAPTURE) together with them in the clouds, to meet the Lord in the air: and so shall we ever be with the Lord" (I Thessalonians 4:16-17).

Second Coming of Christ

This is one of the most prominent doctrines in the Bible. In the New Testament alone it is referred to over 300 times. His First Coming was over 1900 years ago when He came on earth to save man from sin. The Second Coming is an event starting at the Rapture and comprehending four phases: *First,* at the Rapture Christ takes the believers out of this world to be with Him (I Thessalonians 4). *Second,* Christ pours out His judgments on the world during the 7 year Tribulation Period. *Third,* Christ at the end of the 7 year Tribulation destroys the Antichrist and his wicked followers at Armageddon (Revelation 19). *Fourth,* Christ sets up His millennial Kingdom prophesied so often in the Old Testament.

Tribulation

In our reference to the Tribulation Period we mean that period of phenomenal world trial and suffering that occurs during the seven-year reign of Antichrist. Daniel 12:1 tells us, " . . . there shall be a time of trouble, such as never was since there was a nation."

It is at this time that the Jews (and those who accept Christ as Saviour during this seven-year period) will be severly persecuted through imprisonment, torture and death.[1]

[1] Some scholars reserve the title **"Great Tribulation"** (Matthew 24:21), for only the latter half of this seven year period. During this latter half ... the troubles of the period will reach their zenith.

Singapore Bans Large Families

SINGAPORE (AP) — The government announced today it will take action against families who refuse to practice family planning after August 1973.

A Health Ministry policy statement to parliament said that in modern Singapore a third child is a luxury and fourth and fifth child are "anti-social acts."

Families with more than two children will get lower priority for public housing

 "The only hope for future generations to enjoy a satisfactory quality of life is to limit human population."

International Symposium
"Uniting Nations for BioSurvival"
United Nations Conference on the Human Environment
Stockholm, Sweden, 1972

This week there are 2 million more Americans than there were 12 months ago! Although the national birth rate in the United States has been declining in the last 10 years, the fact still remains that the U.S. is still growing by more than 1% a year. At this rate there will be almost 300 million people in this country by the year 2000. Presently there are a little over 200 million people in the U.S. In New York City and Los Angeles the population is shooting up even faster than it is in India! In Christ's day there were 200 million people on earth. Today, 1973, over 3,500 MILLIONS! It is estimated that by the year 2000 there will be approximately 6 billion people living on the earth! Even if the population of this world did not increase by one single person...the sad fact is that even now **we cannot cope even with our present population.** We cannot meet the human needs of food and shelter. We cannot live in peace.

One of the present problems, which over the next few years will become increasingly severe, is that mankind is not uniformly distributed over the face of the Earth.

If we could spread out our population evenly we would have 65 people per square mile of land area on the Earth. Today's United States population, if spread uniformly within the continental U.S., would put 55 people per square mile. The present population of Japan, evenly distributed over that mountainous land, would make 700 people per square mile. But because populations tend to be denser in urban (city) areas, the figures below more accurately portray the true nature of the present population problem.

Tokyo	20,000 people per square mile
New York City	25,000 people per square mile
Manhattan	75,000 people per square mile

And what is Tokyo doing to resolve their population density? Moving out of the city? No. Tokyo is using 7000 tons of garbage a day to fill Tokyo Bay...to expand! Tokyo right now has approximately 17 million people. It is expected to reach 40 million people by the year 2000!

Population pressures cause war. China will have to expand or starve. India adds more *annually* to its population than the entire population of Australia today.

I PREDICT by 1982

Population densities coupled with air pollution will cause great waves of air stagnation in New York City, Los Angeles and Tokyo. Pockets of oxygen depletion will have become so serious by this time that...an epidemic of sudden deaths will result. Governments will be shocked into taking radical steps to remedy the situation. Alaska will become America's new frontier.

The federal income tax system will allow tax exemptions for only the first **three** children—thereby attempting to discourage larger families.

Too Many People Too Fast Spells Disaster in Year 2000

Billions of People

0   1   2   3   4   5   6

2000
6.1 billion
people

NOW
3.8 billion
people

1939
World War II
2.2 billion
people

1914
World War I
1.7 billion
people

1848
California
Gold Rush
1.1 billion
people

1776
Declaration of
Independence
850 million
people

1492
Columbus
Discovers
America
400 million
people

1215
Magna Carta
350 million
people

476
Fall of Roman
Empire
290 million
people

Birth of Christ
250 million
people

10

TIMETABLE TO TROUBLE

There is an average of 55 Americans per square mile! By the year 2000 there will be about 87 Americans per square mile.

Holland now has almost 1000 people per square mile, Japan...700 and West Germany...600.

New Jersey is the state with the most people per square mile in the world! Regardless of all the methods being attempted to control births ...abortion, birth control pills...they will not be successful. The populations of all countries will continue to grow. Births will still surpass deaths. Some claim that only one method of control will work: forced sterilization, forced abortions. So called "action groups" are already discussing these alternatives. And only an Antichrist would have the power to enforce such restrictions.

Even if one did not accept the Scriptures but based his conclusions on scientific facts and trends one could see that the world is heading for disaster, riots, anarchy, dictatorships and a holocaust of frightful proportions!

Let's look at our own "abundant" United States.

Because we may be well-fed and have most of our needs met, we tend to believe that most of America is living in abundance.

Pictured on the right is a new Food Coupon.

Is this the first step towards The Mark?

By July, 1973, TEN MILLION AMERICANS will be using such stamps to buy food! In fact, **in less than one year** the number of Americans receiving food stamps has **more than doubled** to 8 MILLION people!

In 1969 the nation's welfare rolls swelled to an additional 20% to a record 12,200,000 persons. It is estimated that this will grow to over **14** million people by mid-1973. To administer this food program just for ONE MONTH costs over $115 MILLION. And just to administer the food program in the year 1972 Congress appropriated over **$1.5 BILLION**.

I predict that by the end of 1974 one American in every 20 will be relying on food stamps for part of their food supply.

What does this mean? More and more people will be relying on the U.S. Government to resolve their needs. And because of this the Government will be able to exercise more control over the movements and life pattern of each individual. It is not a question of whether one is for or against this. It is a situation brought about by the population explosion, and by this computerized age which has reduced the necessary labor force at a time when more people are eligible to work. THIS will yet lead to an increase in drug-taking, more unrest, more lawlessness with the law being unable to cope with the situation. Can you now see how those who do not accept some form of allegiance (such as a Mark) will be refused food in deference to those loyal to the Leader?

The Philadelphia Inquirer

WEDNESDAY MORNING, SEPTEMBER 8, 1971   3

Bonuses Urged for Low-IQ Sterilization

PHILIP MEYER   "arthritis" and other   intelligence tests a

U. S. 'May Have to Curb Births'

The population explosion means the American government eventually will have to decide whether to coerce its citizens into having fewer children, White House Counselor Donald Rumsfeld said.

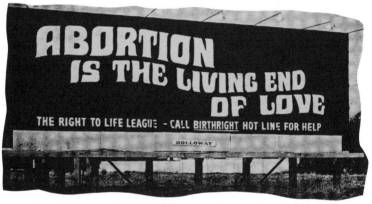

THE NEW YORK TIMES

CONTROLS ASKED ON BIRTHS BY POOR

Michigan Legislator Urges Larger Affluent Families

Special to The New York Times

CHARLEVOIX, Mich., May 6 — A conservative Republican Michigan legislator has proposed the encouragement of an increase in the birth rate among educated, propertied United States citizens and a curbing of births "in America's slums."

New U. S. Office To Cite Perils of Population Rise

WASHINGTON (UPI). — The population of the United States reached 208.5 million on New Year's Day. The Census Bureau believes it will climb to 300 million by the year 2000 and more than 400 million by 2042.

Taking note of this trend, the administration is organizing an Office of Population Education to inform children in school and adults through television about na...

MORALS and
THIS CHANGING WORLD

The above advertisement appeared in a weekly newspaper in Philadelphia in July, 1972!

The individual placing the ad was not serious but did it as a scientific "stunt." He received hundreds of local calls as well as calls from Canada and Europe. He also received over 16 bags of mail!

While the ad offered a $10,000 **+** fee for the woman selected...many women wanted to perform the service free.

I PREDICT such events will become commonplace within the next 2 years.

I PREDICT you will see RENT-A-MOTHER ads flourishing in your local newspapers very shortly.

Right before your very eyes, you are seeing Bible prophecy come alive!

Rent-a-Mother Seen Medically Possible

BIRMINGHAM, England (UPI).—An embryologist suggested today that someday "host mothers" might be paid to give birth to babies conceived in test tubes from the eggs of women unable to have children.

| Allen's attempt to have a baby

New Set of Morals, Family Shift Seen in Next 3 Decades

By GAY PAULEY

NEW YORK (UPI).—The 1960s brought right on ... have the Victorians reeling in their gra--- onto stage and screen. New ...

All this "revol--- the decade of the dec--- swer: A sw--- new pattern o--- new set of mo--- three decades.

Sex, just fo--- sake, will be r--- come instead a ... live act with an ...

A LEARNED of sex by the ye...

Love for Sale: Firm Operating Brothels Looks for Investors

* * *

A Bordello Owner in Germany ... ... Available;

erotica that would ... ... and acts moved ... and act, of youth.

independent, tightly urban organiza- ... have for a soci- ... of private indi- ... personal feel- ... will be found in marriage of two

... ithout this level ... nd honest com- ... th another fel- ... are less than an individual

This is not a poorly printed picture. It is an **actual** photograph taken by the author in Tokyo at noon. There was not one cloud in the sky. The sun was shining. Yet, because of the polluted air, very little of the sunlight reaches the earth in Tokyo!

"The ultimate solution...is man's breakout from planet earth...to seed the distant planets and still more distant stars so that they become habitable for human beings."

C. L. Sulzberger
New York Times

The earth is basically a closed system! The winds that ventilate the earth are a little over 6 miles high. Above this level the air rapidly thins out to almost nothingness by the 15 mile level.

And more and more we are rapidly filling every inch of air space in this limited 15 mile umbrella that covers the world. This area where life exists is called the biosphere. Life on earth is maintained through a delicate balance of elements. We are rapidly upsetting this balance. Here are some examples of areas that may trigger disaster as the world continues to run out of earth:

1. Each year the United States alone ploughs under and paves over 1,000,000 acres of oxygen-producing trees.

2. We are burying ourselves under 7 million scrapped cars, 30 million tons of waste paper, 48 billion discarded cans and 28 billion bottles and jars a year!

3. The air we breathe circles the earth 40 times a year, and America contributes to this cycle 140 million tons of pollutants. In fact, 90 million tons of pollutants come from cars alone, with Americans burning more gasoline than all the rest of the world combined.

4. Our world's supply of fossil fuels—coal, petroleum and natural gas—is becoming critical, and shortages are occurring already.

5. The pollutants we have hurled into the sky year upon year are now raining their verdict of death upon us. The 406-year-old North Rhineland village of Knapsack, Germany is probably the first town in history to be declared officially unfit for human habitation because of air pollution. This occurred in July, 1972.

6. Not only are we running out of earth, but we are also running out of oceans. Pollutants are choking the world's seas. The bottom half of the Baltic sea is already dead!

7. Airline pilots report that poisonous pollutants shroud almost every U.S. city, including remote towns like Missoula, Montana. Apollo 10 astronauts could see Los Angeles as a cancerous smudge from 25,000 miles away in outer space!

8. Pollutants are already changing weather patterns, and meteorologists are concerned that major cities will soon begin to experience unusually cold or unusually hot temperatures.

I PREDICT by 1990

Tokyo will have no trees.

Our sea level will increase over 12" causing massive coastal flooding.

Thousands will die as smog smothers many cities.

'Red Tide' in New England Costs Thousands of Jobs

The "red tide" causes havoc in Florida.

Some people believe the answer to our problems is exporting people to other planets. If this were possible and we had a spaceship that would hold 100 people...

In order to keep the present population of the Earth **constant** *we would have to export 70 million people per year.*

This would require the launching of 700,000 spaceships per year— or about 2000 spaceships each day! The fantastic cost of such an earth-saving project would be in excess of $300 billion a day. One can see the impossibility of such a plan! Plainly, we are running out of earth and ocean; we are approaching the Earth's Limits.

PREVIEW of the TRIBULATION PERIOD

When some people read of the 2nd Vial and 3rd Vial judgments of Revelation 16...they find such events difficult to imagine.

And yet, right now, we may be seeing the groundwork of such prophecy in the initial stages of fulfillment!

The photograph on the left shows a cleanup crew using pitch forks to load a truck with decomposing fish from the beach near Tampa, Florida. Here, millions of fish died in 1971 in a "red tide" that released a syrupy film which strangled marine life. The sea literally turned red! This is happening NOW!

Four years ago Scandinavian scientists woefully discovered that every part of the Baltic Sea (160,000 square miles) which was deeper than 200 feet was **totally devoid of oxygen!** There were no fish, no snails, no worms. The bottom half of the sea was, in fact, dead!

It was discovered that wildlife are dying in that area with dangerous levels of DDT and mercury in their bodies!

Many doctors feel that pollutants from air and sea are a cause of cancer. Doctors still cannot understand why breast cancer is six times more common in the United States than it is in Japan. Lung cancer occurs seven times more frequently among men in the United Kingdom than among men in India. Experts believe that 80% of human cancers are caused by factors in our environment.

Our once green earth is now casting a grey pall of death as the pollutants in our air, our sea and on our land are slowly suffocating our very existence. And while medical techniques for saving life are far greater than 10 years ago...life expectancy has not increased correspondingly.

We are living in a paradox. We spent 140 times more for death-dealing hardware in Vietnam than we are presently expending to protect those Americans who will die of cancer.

If pollution seems bad in the United States...it is far worse in Japan! Few countries are as heavily polluted as Japan, where 103.5 million people live! One organization estimates that waste generated per square mile in Japan is 10 times greater than in the United States.

School children in Japan have been knocked out by smog. Rivers are unswimmable. Even the best beaches are contaminated. Tokyo police use an oxygen-inhaler after one hour of directing traffic!

What does this mean? Within the next 10 years you will see drastic changes in our living pattern. Look for more illnesses...erratic behavior patterns caused by chemically laden air spewed from auto exhaust systems...much tragedy!

17

Mother in Tokyo examines oxygen-producing machine at gift counter in department store.

Tokyo Combats a New Pollutant, Pockets of Oxygen-Deficient Air

Rescue squad pulling up dead Japanese workmen trapped in pockets of oxygen-deficient air.

Christianity Linked to Pollution

By EDWARD B. FISKE
Special to The New York Times

CLAREMONT, Calif., April 30 —A group of Protestant theologians asserted here today that Christianity had played its part in provoking the current environmental crisis and that any solution to it would

Scholars Cite Call in Bible for Man to Dominate Life

major paper of the conference. "Individually and collectively we should rapidly

be the object of the same love that is directed to human beings.

The theologian said that because it was impossible for people to "believe something simply because it seems advantageous to believe it," a change

Pennsylvania National Guardsmen and Harrisburg City Police board an Armored Personnel Carrier in Harrisburg patroling the residential areas to prevent looting in the wake of the flood in which many homes were evacuated.

Winter Storms Kill 8 in Nation; Rain Leaves 63 Dead in Europe

2-Inch Rain Soaks Area;

Tornadoes, Floods Add To Damage

F.P.C. Predicts Shortage Of Natural Gas in Winter

By EDWARD COWAN
Special to The New York Times

WASHINGTON, Nov. 29—The Federal Power Commission reported today that the country's shortage of national gas this winter would be the largest on record and almost twice as large as last winter.

The gravity of the shortage will depend on the weather—

When gas supplies are inadequate, interstate pipelines and local distributors customarily stop deliveries first to factories and utilities and other so-called interruptible customers with capacity to switch to oil or coal.

Capacity to Switch

In New York City and el...

Flood Forces Penna. To Suspend Lottery; Equipment Ruined

By DUKE KAMINSKI
Bulletin Harrisburg Bureau

Harrisburg—Flood damage tickets and equipment...

tion of the lottery and to beef up future prizes.

Computers Wiped Out

ets, the computers and a number of vehicles used to distribute the tickets were...

CHANGING WEATHER PATTERNS
A Preview of Tribulation Chaos

In June, 1972, Hurricane Agnes struck the eastern seaboard affecting 10 million Americans.

The flood caused millions upon millions of dollars in damage in business losses...and perhaps 3 billion dollars in personal losses.

Yet the newspaper headline here pictured is indicative of the concern of some people at the height of this tragedy...the fact that the flood will force Pennsylvania to suspend the state lottery temporarily.

The winter of 1972 witnessed winds blowing in an abnormal weather pattern. It produced an unusual cold winter in the Western states and an unusually mild winter in the Eastern states. Because of this peculiar weather pattern the Atlantic Ocean warmed up as much as 5 degrees.

All over the world meteorologists have been noticing strange weather patterns which have no precedence.

In Sao Paulo, Brazil, the usual 35-degree winters were recently replaced by sunny 80-degree days! Unusual weather will soon be evident in other areas as well.

Hurricane Agnes caused such devastation because its path did not follow the weathermen's predictions. Will future weather patterns now be so erratic so as to defy prediction of their course of destruction?

Can this also be a preview of the chaos that will be prevalent during the Tribulation Period? Are we seeing a foretaste of the disasters that will pit every man against another and each man for himself?

One of the saddest reflections on Hurricane Agnes was the fact that people benefited by the misery of others. The National Guard and local police were kept busy periodically arresting looters who swarmed in on flood areas stealing everything they could get their hands on. Future tragedies will see an increase in such inhuman actions.

Perhaps no photograph expresses so tragically the disaster of the 1972
floods than this one.

These Corning residents were grateful for the supply of fresh water trucked in from Rochester, N.Y. Corning's water supply was contaminated by flood water.

"Water, water, everywhere,
but not a drop to drink."
Samuel Taylor Coleridge
The Rhyme of the Ancient Mariner

Have you ever been on a hot desert where the temperature can soar to 125°? Do you recall the time when Bishop Pike and his wife went driving towards the Dead Sea? They turned off the main road and became stranded. All they had to drink between them was a bottle of soft drink. Bishop Pike was later found dead. The intense heat of the sun coupled with the lack of water was the cause of death.

We take water for granted and lavishly use it as though we were dipping from an inexhaustible source.

Little do we realize how much *fresh* water is needed just to produce the foods and materials we enjoy today. As an example a single corn plant requires as much as 200 quarts of fresh water during its growing season. Here are some other eye-opening statistics:

To produce:		Needed:
1 pound of wheat	-	60 gallons of water
1 pound of rice	-	200 gallons of water
1 pound of meat	-	up to 6000 gallons of water
1 quart of milk	-	1000 gallons of water
1 automobile	-	100,000 gallons of water

In 1900 each American's share of all of the fresh water this nation consumed was 525 gallons a day. Today each American's share is 1500 gallons a day. By the year 2000 it is estimated that each American's share will be 2000 gallons a day.

Where is all this fresh water going to come from?

Of all the water on earth

97% is salt water.

This leaves the 3% which is fresh water. But, of this 3%, 98% of this fresh water (or 2.94% of all the water) is tied up in the ice caps of Antarctica and Greenland.

This leaves 6/100's of 1% which is the fresh water we have available for use! Some have suggested melting the ice caps, but to do this would raise the sea level some 200 feet!

During Hurricane Agnes which struck the East Coast of the United States that same summer, water was being sold to the unfortunate victims at $1 a gallon!

I PREDICT by 1980

You will pay 5 cents for a glass of water in a restaurant.

The water system of a riot-torn city will be infiltrated with a pacifying drug to calm the population.

The quest to convert ocean salt water into fresh water will become a top priority item of major governments. Stocks of water producing companies will be traded on the stock exchanges.

Water quotas will be instituted in the United States. The cost of water beyond any home's or any industry's rationed quota will be triple the cost of water within the quota.

The severe drought that struck Florida in 1972 left some areas a checker-board of cracked, parched earth. We are plagued with either too much water or too little.

POLLUTION IN OCEAN REACHES CRITICAL LEVELS

Representatives of some 35 nations quietly met in London a short time ago to discuss the alarming conditions of the oceans of the world.

Because the oceans of the world have become one gigantic septic tank in which poisonous wastes are accumulating at rates that are alarming, an international effort is being planned to identify the most dangerous changes before it is too late!

Probably close to a quarter of all DDT manufactured to date is now in the oceans and fish worldwide are contaminated. The recent discovery of dangerous mercury in many forms of sea life is but a taste of things to come.

In California alone there are over 50,000 industrial plants that are contributing gross contamination to the sea by discharges of waste products. These plants dump annually 1.8 million gallons of chromium and cyanide compounds as well as other poisonous wastes into the ocean.

What does this mean? People mistakenly believe there is sufficient water in the world to meet our needs. They little realize that we have so polluted our oceans that some people after eating fish have died from a respiratory failure brought about by what is called ciguatera fish poison. In one case it was concluded that the poison passed through the milk of the mother to kill her suckling child.

We are rapidly approaching the Last Days and we have just about depleted our water supply here on earth.

NEARLY EVERYBODY READS THE BULLETIN

The Sunday Bulletin

INDEPENDENT—LOCALLY OWNED

WITH DAILY EVENING EDITION

SECTION ONE

TODAY YEAR, NO. 75 • COPYRIGHT, 1972, BULLETIN CO., PHILADELPHIA, PA. 19105 • 215-582-7600   SUNDAY, JUNE 25, 1972   XJK   ☆ ☆ ☆   35 CENTS

Nixon and Shapp Fly Over Disaster Area; Drinking Water Limited in Phila. Suburbs

Cleanup Starts On Schuylkill; Disease Feared

By HENRY R. DARLING and KARL ABRAHAM
Of The Bulletin Staff

Officials and residents of communities alon...

Floods Kill 42; Damage Set at Over $1 Billion

By BAYARD BRUNT and DUKE KAMINSKI
Of The Bulletin Staff

President Nixon and Governor Shapp flew over

Federal Study's Findings

Hazardous Metals Pollute Water Sources for a Dozen U.S. Cities

By David W. Hacker

There's more than mercury that falls to meet the eye in the nation's streams and lakes. And last fall the U.S. Geological set out to see how much of these showed up in 720 water sam... arsenic, cad... and zinc. ...of the ...red

may be in even higher concentrations. The bottom mud is where the metals might have an even greater effect on fish and wildlife.

The Geological Survey has dispatched its findings to those areas where the arsenic and cadmium readings are at potentially troublesome levels. Said a spokesman: "We've told the state health departments to get busy, do something."

Here are some of the areas, largely whose untreated waters showed

---

57 Murders Here in Week Set Record the Police Link to Heat

By ERIC PACE

Fifty-seven homicides—a record—were committed here in the seven-day period that ended at midnight Thursday, the office of the Chief Medical Examiner reported yesterday.

"That certainly is the greatest number we've ever had in one week," said Dr. Milton Helpern, who joined the office in 1931 and has been the Chief Examiner since 1954. The figure for the same seven days in 1971 was 25, and the average weekly homicide toll last year was 31.

air-conditioner, he's sitting on the stoop, he has a few beers, there's no place to go, he gets mad at something," said Capt. Alfred E. Doran of the crime analysis section. "Then all of a sudden it bursts out into the open: he grabs a knife."

Stabbings accounted for 26 of the 57 homicides, an unusually high proportion. Twenty-four were shootings, five were assaults, one person was set on fire and an 18-month-old... was thrown out...

W YORK TIMES, WEDNESDAY, JANUARY 19, 1972

2 Youths Charged With Plot to Poison Chicago Water

By ANDREW H. MALCOLM
Special to The New York Times

CHICAGO, Jan. 18—The police arrested two youths here today and charged them with conspiracy to commit murder by plotting to poison the city's drinking water and spread deadly diseases throughout the Midwest.

According to State's Attorney ward V. Hanrahan, a police ...tion found that the ...whom was study...

rests were first leaked on a morning radio program station WGN, as thousands of Chicagoans brushed their teeth and drank their morning coffee.

As rumors raced through the city, Mayor Richard J. Daley hastily called a news conference to assure residents that the city's drinking water, which is also pumped to 72 suburbs, was not contaminated and said. "All fear should be dispelled ...mediately."

"The alleged plot was uncovered last week by the Federal Bureau of Investigation during another investigation. Last night in the belief that overt action was "imminent," plainclothesmen, armed with a search warrant, raided an apartment at 6501 North Fairfield Avenue on the city's northwest side.

There they arrested two persons who the police identified as Allan C. Schwander, 19 old, and Steven

Identified at least one substance seized as typhoid bacteria, Mr. Hanrahan said.

He said the youths had allegedly planned to "poison the water supplies and spread deadly diseases in Chicago, Illinois and elsewhere." He declined to specify what other cities might have been...

The police sa...

Continued on Page 7, Column 3 | Continued on Page 40, Column 2 | Continued on Page ...

Muscovites Suffer From Record Heat and Lack of Beer

The growing evidence that much of the water in the United States is impure has provided a great boom for the bottled water producers. Total annual sales now top $100 million!

THE NEW YORK TIMES, TUESDAY, JUNE 13, 1972

In North India Summer, the Choking Dust Is a Relief

By ROBERT TRUMBULL
Special to The New York Times

NEW DELHI, June 12—In the yearly hell of a North India summer, blinding dust storms so thick that all traffic must stop are a welcome phenomenon. For, while they last, the whirling brown clouds blot out the deadly sun.

The choking dust is driven by a hot wind called the loo. Rising from the burning sands of Rajasthan, India's desert state, the loo ravages the vast northern plain with takes the moisture from the heat that dries up rivers, mouth, causes nostrils to crack inside and makes the skin feel on fire.

This year, this season of transcendent misery for hundreds of millions of Indians has taken more than its usual toll of human lives. According to the government radio, and newspaper figures, at least 676 Indians had perished of heat exhaustion or sunstroke up to yesterday in the current month-long siege of extreme high temperatures.

Drinking-Water Shortage

A national news agency has reported that 226 vil-

lages in Uttar Pradesh state, one of the most severely affected, were experiencing an acute shortage of drinking water. Almost 200,000 persons are affected, the agency said.

Water has b... cious com...
cit... ...

mo... ...
for... ...
to a...
from...
pers...
start...
paper...
head of...
"surviva...

Temp...

Howeve... ...monsoon is coming soon, and the temperature that surpassed 120 degrees a few days ago has dropped to 103 in New Delhi during the day, and all the way to 83 at night.

But the monsoon brings its

own problems. At first, the daily rain is a relief, and Indians rush fr... their houses to stan... ...oling shower... ...e extremely ...eans one ...enched in ...ging on ...form so ...ly quick ...oler cli-...fer the ...iscom-

...ly in ...de-...in-...sp ...e a

...earance
...s quickly change
...arance. Along the colonnaded streets of Connaught Place, New Delhi's shopping section, reed curtains called chiks are unrolled between the masonry columns to shade the sidewalks from the evil sun.

The doorways of the older, air-conditioned government buildings, like the red sand-

stone secretariat complex, are shrouded by portable frames of bamboo and a fragrant local grass called khuskhus. The whole contraption, called a khuskhus tattie, is kept drenched with water so that the dry, hot wind, passing through, picks up moisture, bringing the temperature down perceptibly.

A common substitute for air-conditioners, which are beyond the means of most Indians, is a mechanized khuskhus tattie called a "desert cooler," in which the air is driven through the wet grass by an electric fan. At cocktail parties on lawns in New Delhi, a cool breeze is created by placing large electric fans so that they blow across huge cakes of ice on tables.

There is no such thing as going for a drive to cool off —unless, of course, one has one of the rare air-conditioned cars. And automobile windows are kept closed to keep out the hot wind.

Even so, the steering wheel can become so hot that the driver has to wear gloves, and the metal fixtures inside, like the door handles, are too hot to touch.

Water has become a precious commodity in some cities, as well. In the crowded neighborhood around the huge Moslem mosque called the Jama Masjid, a historic shining pink sandstone landmark in the old city of Delhi, venders sell drinking water at about 5 cents for a few swallows poured from a leather bag.

Man selling water from booth on a New Delhi street during heat wave in India, May, 1972. Over 500 deaths were attributed to the heat.

Nixon Orders Freeze on Wages, Prices, Calls for Tax Reductions to Create Jobs

Acts to Protect Dollar Against Speculators

DRIVE TO CUT RED INK IN THE '73 BUDGET

'amiliar: The tide of red ink seems likely to rise to around 35 billions.

posed to spend 246.3 full 3.7 billion less. th

Empty Pockets on a Trillion Dollars a Year

CAN a nation with a trillion-dollar economy be running out of money? That startling question is fore-

come taxes, sales taxes, property taxes, Social Security taxes and "sin" taxes on liquor and cigarettes. Between the tax burden on man and to

If you drive a car, I'll tax the street,
If you try to sit, I'll tax your seat,
If you get too cold, I'll tax the heat,
If you take a walk, I'll tax your feet.

WHY U.S. TREASURY GETS DEEPER IN DEBT ABROAD

Foreign governments are providing much of the credit to run the U. S. Government. America becomes a debtor, as two kinds of deficits soar.

Two factors are related to this startling turnabout—
• The U. S. Government's rapidly ing deficits, producing
Treasury no
in

which ended

Treasury Asks $40-Billion Rise In Debt Limit, to $435-Billion

WASHINGTON, Feb. 17—The
Administration asked Congress
today for a $40-billion increase
in the statutory debt limit—the
largest since the end of World
War II—and for repeal of th

> "We are taxed in our bread, in our incomes and our investments, on our land and on our property...for foreign nations, complacent nations who will bow to us...mendicant nations who will destroy us when we show a moment of weakness or our treasury is bare, and surely it is becoming bare! We are taxed to maintain legions on their soil, in the name of law and order. They take our very flesh, and they hate and despise us. When a government becomes powerful it is destructive, extravagant and violent...."
>
> Cicero, 54 B.C.

32

In 1973
the United States government collected over $246 Billion in taxes from its citizens. If you put this 1973 Federal budget in dollar bills, fastened end to end, you would have a belt of green that could reach around the earth 956 times.

Of this amount, about 1/3rd is allocated for Defense spending. Over $5 billion goes for law enforcement. And paying interest on the national debt is the third largest item in the 1973 budget, $22.7 billion!

By the end of fiscal 1973, the national debt will total $493.2 billion. That comes to $2,374.09 for every American citizen! Or over $850,000 a minute!

Richard Nixon is the first President in the United States to spend a TRILLION DOLLARS while in office. His first budget provided for more than was spent by all Presidents from Washington through the first two terms of Franklin D. Roosevelt, a period of 153 years.

The United States Government is the biggest organization on earth. It employs over 6 million people and pays them over 40 Billion dollars a year. One out of every 13 Americans works for the U.S. Government. And 64,000 U.S. officials make $20,000 to $35,000 a year.

Government spending on the "welfare state" has finally reached a point where it is threatening to drain the U.S. Treasury. In 1955 there were 5,830,000 on relief receiving some $2.7 billion in aid. By 1970 there were over 13 million on relief receiving over $13 billion in aid. This is only one of the problems that year after year brings increasing taxes.

Do you know that there are 151 different taxes on a loaf of bread, 150 on a woman's hat, 600 on a house, and even 100 on an egg!

In 1940 20¢ out of every $1 went for taxes. Today, over 35¢ out of every $1 goes for taxes!

The U.S. national debt totals over $493.2 billion, of which $50 billion is owed outside the U.S. To offset this "external debt," it has only $11 billion in gold and $3 billion in foreign currency.

In reality, the United States is bankrupt.

I PREDICT by 1976

There will be another anti-taxation "Boston Tea Party" that will outdo the original one in 1773.

You will see a dramatic change in government when this occurs.

The government will begin to debate schemes for paying off part of the national debt by the printing up of a few billion dollars worth of "extra" paper money.

Taxpayers all over New York converged on Albany in February, 1971 to protest tax increases called for in Governor Rockefeller's record budget.

The United States now finds itself borrowing billions of dollars from foreign countries to pay for the soaring governmental outlays at home. At one time the U.S. was the world's greatest lender.

In 1969 the U.S. owed foreign government banks only $11 billion or 3% of the U.S. public debt. Today, it owes over $50 billion or 11% of the U.S. public debt. Such growing dependency on foreign nations may one day force the United States to join the United States of Europe.

36¢ out of
every $1
for TAXES

Richard M. Nixon*
1972
$246 BILLION

33¢ out of
every $1
for TAXES

Lyndon B. Johnson
1967
$158 BILLION

32¢ out of
every $1
for TAXES

John F. Kennedy
1962
$107 BILLION

20¢ out of
every $1
for TAXES

Franklin D. Roosevelt
1945
$95 BILLION

Woodrow Wilson
1919
$18 BILLION

Abraham Lincoln
1865
$1.3 BILLION

THE ROAD TO AN
OVER 200-BILLION BUDGET
Paved with the Mounting
Burden of Taxes
from George Washington
to Richard Nixon

James Madison
1814
$35 MILLION

* In 30 years the tax take in the United States has
multiplied 17 times. It has soared from 20% of the
national income in 1940 to 36% of the national
income today. Richard Nixon will be the first President
to spend a trillion dollars while in office. By 1974 the
national debt will exceed $500 BILLION. Interest on
the national debt will become the 3rd largest item on
the budget, $22.7 BILLION (or 150% of the 1941
budget of $14 BILLION).

George Washington
1789-91
$4 MILLION

> *If you drive a car,*
> > *I'll tax the street,*
>
> *If you try to sit,*
> > *I'll tax your seat,*
>
> *If you get too cold,*
> > *I'll tax the heat,*
>
> *If you take a walk,*
> > *I'll tax your feet.*

LOOK OUT FOR A TAX REVOLT

A recent survey showed that 60% of those questioned feel they have reached "the breaking point" on taxes they pay. Americans now pay about 37% of their income on taxes. Form 1040 which once contained only 200 words of "instructions," now requires 3,238 words of instructions! Prophetically, look for more taxes, more control, and a resultant increased federal aid that will make everyone dependent on the government. This could pave the way for Antichrist.

POPULATION POSTER

 "We have made an antiserum that may be the first step in the production of vaccination against fertility."

Andrew Schally
World leader in fertility hormone research

For every child born in America,
the domestic automobile industry will produce 2 additional motor vehicles! The boom in babies has accelerated the sale of toys, baby food and apparel. Shoes and clothes account for about $80 billion in sales yearly.

Should the skids be put on the baby boom, business will have to look elsewhere for profits.

One Michigan legislator in May, 1972 suggested, "There is a need for curbing the growth of the drone population that weakens our society."

A professor at Stanford University suggested the government should pay bonuses to people with heredity defects who volunteer to be sterilized. People who score below the average level of 100 on IQ tests, he said, should get a sterilization bonus of $1000 for each point below 100.

Another writer suggested that there should be a tax penalty of $500 on the birth of the third, fourth and fifth child, etc. And tax deductions of $1000 per year should be given for the man who has a vasectomy.

In Holland they have already perfected a unisex contraceptive that can be used by either male or female to prevent conception.

And the U.S. government has organized an Office of Population Education to inform children in school and adults through television about the adverse effects of population growth. The initial budget available for this was set at approximately $5 million.

Students on many campuses are recruiting supporters for ZPG, Zero Population Growth.

Recently from 23 countries family planners came to the United Nations July, 1972 to pool ideas on how to halt unchecked population growth.

Birth control by vaccination will soon be a reality! Three of four different approaches are being researched. No doubt, within a short time ...such a vaccination will not only be feasible but will be put into practice.

Singapore announced it will take action against families who refuse to practice family planning...terming the fourth and fifth child as "antisocial acts."

I PREDICT by 1981

Pregnancy in many countries will be by Permit. Individuals will be vaccinated at an early age to prevent pregnancy. If one passes a mental test and a health test, a permit will be issued and an antidote administered so that one pregnancy can be fulfilled by that individual.

A NEW MOVEMENT CHALLENGES THE U.S. TO STOP GROWING

ZPG

Birth Control by "Litmus Test"

A simple saliva test may soon be on tap to help take the gamble out of the "rhythm method" of birth control. According to Raymond O. Foster, a research chemist at Weston Laboratories, Ottawa, Illinois, there is a cyclic increase in the activity of a chemical in saliva that coincides with an increase in body temperature. As it happens, a rise in temperature is a fairly reliable indication of ovulation.

Your National Wildlife Federation in Action...
HOPES OF WORLD REST ON LIMITING FUTURE HUMAN POPULATION

---

38 M   *food fashions family furnishings*   THE NEW YORK TIMES, TUESDAY, JANUARY 12, 1971

To Them, Two Children Are Fine, but Three Crowd the World

By JUDY KLEMESRUD

Mrs. Shirley Lewis raised two fingers in the V-shaped peace sign yesterday and said she has had her own meaning for the gesture.

"It means, 'Stop at Two,'" the slender, red-haired woman said, smiling.

Mrs. Lewis, who is the wife of a pediatric intern, was one of four leaders of the New York chapter of Zero Population Growth who met yesterday to talk about the relatively new and rapidly growing population control group.

since it was founded early in 1969, she said, and most of them spent the group's bureau. A black-and-white number with the letters "ZPG" sitting on top of what looks like a road map, but is actually a statistical graph. The graph is supposed to symbolize what will happen if the world's population continues at its present rate (such a population explosion would have dire consequences), 2291 before 1975, or if there is zero population growth a stabilized population).

"We're mad against children or babies at all," said

unimpressive headquarters— a portion of an artist's loft on the eighth floor of 722 Broadway. The walls are decorated with graphs, charts, posters and slogans such as: "Stop at Two!", "Make Love, Not Babies!" "Smaller Families or Bigger Headaches!", and "Anyone Can Have a Baby. A Baby. A Baby. A Baby. A Baby. Is It Worth Repeating?"

"What we're saying is that if people stop at two now, the population will stabilize by the year 2010," said Judy Senderowitz, 29, chairman of the 800-member New York chapter, who works at headquarters.

couples want three or more children.

"Even if we continue at our present 1 per cent growth rate, which demographers say is the lowest since the Depression," she added, "our population will still double in 85 years. And that means we will have to double our schools, hospitals, fire departments and social services."

Probably nothing makes ZPG people angrier than to see pictures of large families in advertisements or newspaper and magazine articles. When this happens, ZPG'ers fire off irate letters to the advertising agencies and the

Population Control Can Improve Nation's Quality of Life

> "The commission believes that slowing the rate of population growth would ease the problems facing the American government in the years ahead."
>
> —The Commission on Population Growth and the American Future

Because of the pervasive impact of population growth on every facet of American life and its implications for the quality of life, the commission has concluded that the nation has come for the United States to adopt a deliberate population policy.

The United States today has a declared no-growth, low population policy, except for open space, and population leaving its control effect, but that does not eliminate the on-the population.

The commission believes that slowing the rate of population growth would ease the problems facing the American government in the years ahead

Even a small difference in average family size makes an enormous difference over the decades. A century from now, with continued immigration, the two-child average would result in a population of 340 million, while growth at the three-child level would result in nearly a billion.

Above all, the commission wishes to emphasize that the alleviation of the problems we have discussed does not depend upon the attainment of no increase in the population.

improve the quality of education for particular individuals throughout the nation.

The Federal Government should enact a Population Education Act to assist school systems in establishing well-planned population education programs.

cial, and institutional pressures that historically have encouraged childbearing, as well as to equalize opportunities for children, we should develop

preferences in childbearing and family size, we should

Increase investment in the search for improved means by which individuals may control their own fertility.

Extend subsidized family-planning programs.

Liberalize access to abortion services, with the admonition that abortion not be considered a primary means of fertility control.

Extend and improve the delivery of health services related to fertility—including prenatal and pediatric care, contraceptive services, voluntary sterilization, abortion, and the treatment of infertility—through public and private financing mechanisms.

In order to regulate the impact on population of migration from outside this country, we should not increase

---

Thursday, Nov. 16, 1972 Philadelphia Inquirer   19

More Couples Are Making a Bold Decision: No Children for Us

By MARILYNN MARTER

No other reason there is no long-lasting, for us could never mentally, emotionally and environmentally fit to reproduce.

There are trial marriages, but no trial children.

More and more couples are becoming concerned with the "why" of having children, rather than the "why not?"

AND HARRY had

years. Harry, 29, recently had a vasectomy.

"We decided we just couldn't handle raising a family," said Sandy, 23, who works as a secretary. "It wouldn't be fair and we felt we just couldn't, and has realized one reason: 'I'm a married mate and Harry's an engineer and we're both involved with our jobs. It's not that we don't like children, we really just like to take trips.

"We never really thought about it until I got pregnant and lost the baby. We then we had made up our mind that

> "I haven't seen that many couples that are really happy with children. More often than not, husbands will say they're sorry they had children, that it spoiled a good thing."
>
> —Marcie Lake

abortion. He is used at all levels to help decide who to raise.

THROUGH THEIR friends and family ties and kind of the kind to people who don't have any, who, especially

those who have children, who always say, Well, have a child It's wonderful to have a child to fulfill your needs." She kind of feels that some where you'd act like he is all things I have no need. But now Sandra says just before

THE NUMBER of couples choosing to remain childless is increasing in wave again. In 24 the percentage with no children and during its children here increased from 13 percent in 1971 to 14 percent in 1972, of whom once 29-30

the percentage has increased from 22 percent to 10 percent.

In a study of the changing views towards childlessness by Dr. Edward Pohlman, professor of counseling psychology at the College of the Pacific taken among 186 college students in 1963 and 100 in 1970, the per centage showing no children increased from 4 to 6 percent, those desiring one child went from 1 percent to 1 percent, those desiring two children increased from 2 percent to six percent and those desiring

three or more children went from 40 percent to 30 percent.

A study of 200 high school students in Cupertino, Cal., September, 1972, comparing their attitudes with the practice of their own parents showed that where 75 percent of the parents had three or more children, identity more than 73 percent of the students indicated a desire for two or fewer children. 17.7 percent of those desiring to remain childless.

PSYCHOLOGISTS give many reasons for wanting children—sincerely taking

ELLEN PECK
. . . a free choice?

'We W

"BAN THE BABIES" Trend Growing Rapidly

In August, 1972, Zero Population Growth (an organization dedicated to stabilizing the population of the United States by 1990) opened an office in Philadelphia.

Nationally, ZPG claims over 25,000 members.

A recent report of the National Wildlife Federation to its members stated, "HOPES OF WORLD REST ON LIMITING FUTURE HUMAN POPULATION."

The 1972 meeting of the UN Conference on the Human Environment made this declaration:

"The only hope for future generations to enjoy a satisfactory quality of life is to limit human population."

And on July 15, 1972 family planners met at the UN from 23 countries to pool ideas on how to halt unchecked population growth. In 1971 India reported they had successfully sterilized 2.1 million people and they are working for a liberal abortion law.

And in England, Baroness Summerskill, speaking in the House of Lords, commented: "Has the time arrived when there should be a revision of the marriage service with the object of reminding married couples that indiscriminate procreation of children, far from being encouraged by the church, is to be condemned as anti-social?" She went on to say, "The sooner the service is amended the better it will be for the nation."

What does this mean?

Watch for Christians to be persecuted and blamed for the population explosion. The first step will be an attempt at persuasion through the clergy to change marriage vows. Education through television commercials and through schools...now being practiced....will become more insistent. While this will have some measure of success, the population will continue to zoom. Then, finally governments will step in with economic incentives, quota systems for births and birth control vaccinations! These are the Last Days!

PREDICTIONS and Comments...

July 1, 1970...abortions were made legal in New York State. In just 6 short months, in **New York City** alone over 100,000 women received abortions in the city's 18 municipal hospitals! At least 26 of the fetuses aborted were born alive. Only one lived. **I PREDICT** that in the year 1973 there will be over ONE-HALF MILLION abortions performed in New York City and over ONE MILLION in the entire state. Such practice will gain wide acceptance and more states will adopt these liberal laws.

NEWS ARTICLE GIVES FORETASTE of COMING ANTICHRIST RULE

In the editorial section of the New York TIMES on December 15, 1970 there appeared a 30" article on birth control.

The headline read:

> WE MUST LIMIT FAMILIES BY LAW
> Population Explosion
> Demands Compulsory
> Birth Control Now

The photograph on the left appeared with this article.

Here are some of the excerpts from that article:

"The voluntary system of birth control has shown little progress relative to time, effort, and money put into it...There is no substitute for a strong over-all policy to thwart the individual license to over-propagate...The prevention of overconcentration of people—though rarely mentioned—is in itself a major problem. The longer Congress tolerates this non-policy drift, the harder, costlier, and less reversible it becomes."

The article continues:

"The present loose system of voluntary family planning...is risky in effectiveness and time...The ultimate necessity of legislation and guidelines for a strong population policy must be faced. Elected officials can no longer evade debating the ideologic issue of whether the individual right to procreate, to the detriment of society, is a basic human right and a fundamental freedom and whether it can be legally halted without damaging the fabric of freedom...There seems to be every moral and philosophical justification for legal population limitation..."

This article was written by Dr. Edgar Berman, research surgeon, who served as special assistant on health problems for Vice President Hubert H. Humphrey.

There have been several articles appearing in national publications written in the same vein as this. Such a procedure generally paves the way for a drastic announcement...that of controlling population. One step in this direction has been the approval of abortion by several states...and the encouraging of such practice. This will not be enough, however to stem the tide of overpopulation.

What next? **I PREDICT** that before 1980 there will be definite laws on the books of the United States prohibiting families from having more than 3 children. Those that do will be penalized by paying more income tax (receiving less deductions). I also PREDICT this system will not be sufficient. The next step will be to sterilize males after two children.

There will be even more drastic steps taken. The Government will eventually have more control over each individual life...thus paving the way for a dictatorship government under Antichrist. Never before has so much happened so quickly!

An old East Pakistan refugee woman dying by the roadside near Calcutta is fanned by another refugee to provide some comfort before death.

"Horses are fed bran, fiber and other natural foods...probably a better diet than most Americans are getting."

Dr. Denis Burkitt

As many as 1½ billion people in the world are either undernourished or malnourished.

From a standpoint of affluence, the people of the United States are the most malnourished in the world. Since the advent of highly processed foods and the fast food fare America's nutrition has taken a nose dive. The hamburgers with the spongy, soggy rolls coupled with those indigestible french fries are among the major culprits. One hamburger chain cranks out 5 million a day through their over 2000 restaurants. Heart attacks and strokes were not a major cause of death in Japan... until U.S. businesses inundated that country with convenience foods and gooey American pastries.

Mothers-to-be and young children fed on this fare add to the health problems. A child's body grows to only 20% of its adult size in the first 3 years. His brain, however, grows to 80% of its adult size in these same 3 years.

When, because of famine conditions, or improper diet, the child is not properly fed in these first 3 formative years...the brain virtually stops growing. Regardless of how well the child is fed after these first 3 years...he cannot ever completely regain the brain cells lost in those first 3 years.

The result: the child grows up to be a maladjusted, erratic adult. And since the advent of fast fare foods, we have seen riots, unrest, increased crime...due, quite possibly to some extent, because of poor diet in those first 3 formative years.

By 1980 "no-meat" meats and "no-fish" fish (soy protein products) will have become a $2 billion market.

Many people consider the oceans of the world to be an unlimited source of food. This is a myth. 90% of the ocean and nearly 3/4ths of the earth's surface is essentially a biological desert!

The years ahead spell critical food shortages and increasing famine. Already 10 million people die of hunger every year!

I PREDICT by 1987

The earth will be unable to feed its population and many will be subsisting on synthetic foods made from amino acids, carbohydrates, vitamins...some processed from petroleum products.

Peace on earth will be threatened as starving populations listen with itching ears to revolutionary demagogues who will demand by-threat-of-terror food from the "fatter" nations.

THE POLLUTION OF FOOD

The food industry uses 3,000 additives in the convenience foods that consumers demand. Are we injuring ourselves to save 15 minutes at the stove?

Synthetic Meats in Your Diet?

By PATRICIA McBROOM

Dr. Altschul said Americans could readily achieve
~~medically recommended low levels of fats and cholesterol~~

Lead Peril Feared in Canned Baby Milk

By DOLORES KATZ
Knight Newspapers Writer

ATLANTIC CITY. — Babies fed canned evaporated milk or commercially-prepared infant formulas may be in danger of accumulating lead in their bodies, according to researchers at the Connecticut State Department of Health.

The study, presented Monday at the annual meeting of the American Public Health Association, said that babies fed evaporated milk or commercially-prepared formula would have a lead intake of more than 150 parts per million a day.

cially-prepared infant formula, homogenized cow milk and human breast milk.

Lamm, now a pediatrician at New York City's Albert Einstein College of Medicine, said the higher lead content in the canned preparations is probably a result of lead from the can dissolving into the milk.

THE FEDERAL government has not yet established standards for lead content in milk. However, Britain has set a maximum limit for lead in all baby food of .50 parts per million.

Lamm said the ...

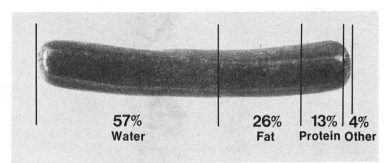

57%
Water

26%
Fat

13%
Protein

4%
Other

The hot dog has been deteriorating since 1928. It now consists of about 57% water, color agents, filler and miscellaneous debris and 26% fat. In fact the Food and Drug Administration said in one report that 40% of the food processing plants they inspected were found to operate under unsanitary conditions. Besides this sad fact, we are eating over 3000 additives from the methyl cellulose in imitation jellies and jams to the BHT and BHA put into our breakfast cereals.

Horses, dogs and cats are probably eating better than most people in the United States.

One philosopher gave this word of advice to his friends:

> Eat breakfast like a king
> lunch like a prince
> dinner like a pauper.

Unfortunately most Americans don't follow this advice, and while our medical care grows more sophisticated, our need for medical care increases.

RUNAWAY RELIEF!

Never before have relief roles been so high, with soaring costs, and no end in sight!

With more people on relief, depending on governmental agencies for their life support, one can see how easily they can be manipulated by an unscrupulous leader.

Let's look at some of the facts:

Government spending in meeting relief roles in America has reached a point where it is actually threatening to bankrupt the States, the cities and drain the U.S. Treasury with chronic federal deficits!

By 1974 it has been estimated that **more than half** of the money U.S. taxpayers contribute to the U.S. Government through taxes...will go towards social welfare spending!

But this fact is even more shocking: There is no evidence that all of this social welfare spending has raised the educational level of these poor people, nor has it lifted them out of a dependency status where they can become productive citizens!

On the contrary, recent experience show that there is a stampede to get on the receiving end of these government handouts...to even demand more government aid as a "legal right." Statistics show that second, third and even fourth generations of welfare families in this country are living on relief as a permanent way of life.

In New York City alone, 1 out of every 6 persons is now on relief. In Newark, New Jersey, almost 1 out of 3 is on relief!

The number of persons on welfare has increased **far more rapidly** than the growth in population. In the last decade nationwide population growth was 13%.

But look at this: In that same period, welfare rolls went up 94%!

In 1960, the total relief benefits amounted to 3.7 billion dollars. In 1970, this figure had grown to 12.8 billion dollars!

Right now there are over 13 million people on relief...costing $12.8 billion a year to maintain!

I PREDICT! By 1975, at least 10% of the nation will be on relief. The annual welfare bill will reach 30 billion dollars!

Medical care for the needy was $492 million in 1960, then it jumped to $5 billion in 1970, and it will soar to $8 billion by 1980.

Look for an avalanche of unrest by 1975 with greater and greater control by the Government over human lives.

Millions of Arab refugees still live in impoverished surroundings, victims of the Arab-Israeli wars. The author took this photograph at a camp near Amman, Jordan. Both Israel and the Arab nations alike will have to seek an equitable solution to this problem before there can be any semblance of peace. For famine-like conditions can fan the flames of a new war.

A $2 bet made by Mayor Lindsay helped get the country's first system of legal offtrack betting off to a flying start in New York City, April 1971.

In 1971 state lotteries became popular with Massachusetts, New Hampshire, New York, New Jersey, Connecticut and Pennsylvania. The founding fathers of these states fought against "gaming" (gambling) as a vice...antagonistic to hard work and thrift. Their office-holding counterparts today, however, manage big gambling industries.

 "There is no doubt in my mind that California will eventually adopt a lottery. It would gross easily $80 million a year."
State Senator, California

Rome, which experienced a rise and fall, had only one Colosseum. The United States...which may yet have a fall...has built dozens! In New Orleans, the Louisiana Superdome seats 80,000 people. Its cost...over $130 million with an expected annual deficit of about $10 million which the state will pick up. In the January, 1972 Super Bowl football fans booked motel rooms within a 60-mile radius 6 months in advance. They spent $10 million in 3 days! The February Mardi Gras added another $21 million spent by a luxury-crazed America.

During a season, a typical pro football team will spend some $120,000 for doctor and hospital bills and another $20,000 for tape, bandages and other supplies. This represents a medical bill for the National Football League's 26 teams of about $3.6 million. And all this for the fans!

In the February, 1972 Hawaiian Open Golf tournament, 12 color cameras were used to televise the event, which was beamed from the Comsat Earth Station on the island of Oahu 22,300 miles to a satellite in "parking orbit" near the equator, then back to another Comsat station in California.

And in October, 1971, Disney World—a $400 million amusement complex—opened on a 27,400-acre site near Orlando, Florida. In its first year of operation over 10 million people visited Disney World. Ground near the area is now selling at over $130,000 an acre!

And when "The Godfather," a motion picture, was introduced in March, 1972, it was grossing $1 million a day at the box office.

While on television, such programs as "All in the Family," were commanding from sponsors $83,000 a minute for commercial time!

Americans, with more free time, more spare cash, have ignited a "leisure boom" that would put the Romans to shame! In 1965 some $58 billion was spent on leisure...in 1972, over 105 billion!

Over 40 million people enjoy three-week vacations. In 1971 a federal law provided five three-day week-ends each year.

Over 2 million Americans today own second homes—used for vacationing. Las Vegas, the small desert gambling mecca, attracts more tourists each year than the combined total of New York City, Hawaii and Florida...and yet its resident population is only 200,000 people.

Meanwhile a strata of socialites plunk down $10,000 to $18,000 to one individual who specializes solely in organizing parties! Pleasure... pleasure...fun...fun...fun.

I PREDICT by 1985 Americans will in one year spend $300 billion on leisure. The 3-day work week will be introduced. There will be more tourists visiting Greece than that country's 8 million population.

Frazier, Ali to Fight March 8
In N. Y. for $2.5 Million Apiece

Expected

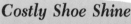

; Penna. Liquor Bill to Hit $10 Million

9 Million Have Drinking Problem

PHILIP MEYER

DR. MERLIN DUVAL

Costly Shoe Shine

IF $2 SOUNDS steep for a shoe shine, think of what else the price includes: about five minutes to talk with or simply watch the three shoe-shine girls, who are naked above the waist. They work at a topless shoe-shine parlor in Baltimore, a place that has been very busy since its opening a couple of weeks ago.

Seventy-two girls responded to classified advertisements for the shoe-shining jobs. The six chosen are housewives, former secretaries, and a former school teacher. "We wanted the best," says one of the shop's three owners. "We couldn't afford to hire hustler-type girls." The job pays $4 an hour plus tips, and there is to be no soliciting.

There is to be conversation, though, and the girls make real efforts to talk with their customers. Some customers do converse. Others are speechless.

52

The Paradox of Life
LOVERS OF PLEASURE

2nd Timothy, chapter 3 views how the world will be in the Last Days. Take time to read it now. You will see it is a clear indication of the days in which we live!

Men, today, are more concerned with pleasure than with the afflictions of millions around them. By 1980, 30% of our income will be spent on luxuries and amusement.

It's the modern day picture of Nero fiddling while Rome burns.

In the middle of devastating Hurricane Agnes...and the mounting problem of feeding refugees throughout the world...much of the world's attention was focused on an event in Reykjavik, Iceland...a CHESS GAME. The tournament between America's Bobby Fischer and Russia's Boris Spassky received front page news coverage.

A stonemason was hired to produce a chess board especially for this game...made from marble squares.

The first one he made was rejected. It was too shiny.
The second one he made was rejected. It was too light...lacked contrast.
The third one he made was rejected. The squares were too big.

Fischer's chair was uncomfortable. He had his own chair flown in to Iceland from New York!

The prize money was not sufficient.

An English millionaire came up with an additional $150,000 making a total of about $300,000 in prize money.

The overhead lights were not satisfactory even though $5,500 had been expended in setting them up. This had to be changed.

The mahogany table for the match, which cost several thousand dollars, was not satisfactory. A carpenter was called in to shorten it.

And WHILE all this was going on...pathetic millions of Americans lived in temporary shelters...their houses, their belongings all lost in a flood and thousands of people throughout the world died of HUNGER. This is a picture of the Last Days! YOU ARE LIVING IN IT. IT IS TAKING PLACE RIGHT BEFORE YOUR EYES!

New York Times

Sodom on the Hudson

There was a time not too many years ago when New York City was relatively innocent of the kind of blatant public vice usually associated with the sleazier areas of London, Hamburg, Tokyo or Paris. There was always commercial sin in the city, of course, but most of it was conducted with some discretion, well away from the mid-Manhattan tourist, restaurant and theater district. But then starting some ten years ago, the scene began to change. First came the prostitutes. They seemed to arrive initially in squad or platoon force, then by battalions, finally in such numbers that they constituted an invading army. In Times Square, and all along Broadway, the whores patrolled in solid phalanx, a grotesquely garbed legion of slatterns who hawked their wares insolently while their pimps oversaw the proceedings from waiting autos. The police arrested dozens of prostitutes nightly, but most were free on bail and at work again in a matter of hours.

Squalid: The inevitable results were not long in manifesting themselves. The whores fought among themselves. Muggings and stabbings of passers-by and potential customers became commonplace. Ordinary citizens, thoroughly frightened, began to shun mid-Manhattan after dark. Business fell off sharply in the area's bars and restaurants, and pacing all this was the growth of an entire apparatus of commercial vice that came in train of the prostitutes. Pornography shops, peep shows, massage parlors, homosexual movie houses and group-sex exhibitions opened and flourished. Police began to suspect that the whole enterprise was linked to organized crime. By early this year, a few blocks of central Manhattan had become as pruriently squalid a place as there is in the nation.

Finally, starting two weeks ago, came

Newsweek, July 26, 1971

WASHINGTON (UPI). — Restaurant-bars in the nation's capital have quietly gone the way of entertainment in San Francisco and other swinging cities and introduced topless dancers.

Within walking distance of the White House and of Attorney General John N. Mitchell's Justice Department, bare-breasted go-go girls — perhaps by emulating — followed suit," Bishop said. "Maybe business was getting bad."

Washington, he said, has about 60 restaurants where go-go girls dance, in various stages of undress, to gyrating music. About half of the places have girls with pasties, Bishop said.

Washington attracts some 17 could disrobe down to pasties and a G-string, but no further.

An official of the district's Alcoholic Beverage Control Board said that there have been no "test" cases of the new bare-breasted dancers. Why?

"Well, the police haven't made any arrests," he said.

Liz' Party Baubles Set at $3 Million

Elizabeth Taylor will wear $3 million worth of diamonds when she goes to a party in Paris Thursday night, a spokesman for the actress said.

Along with Miss Taylor and the diamonds will go a heavy police escort to surround the Chateau de Ferriere estate where **Baron Guy de Rothschild** is giving the party, the spokesman said.

The theme of the event is "Mar-

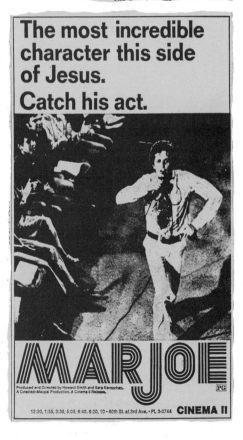

The most incredible character this side of Jesus. Catch his act.

MARJOE

PG

Produced and Directed by Howard Smith and Sarah Kernochan.
A CineVest-Maxpal Production. A Cinema 5 Release.

12:20, 1:55, 3:30, 5:05, 6:40, 8:20, 10 • 60th St. at 3rd Ave. • PL 3-0744   **CINEMA II**

54

Knievel Safe as He Fails To Rocket Over Canyon

TWIN FALLS, Idaho, Sept. 8
—Evel Knievel failed today in
an attempt to rocket ____ feet
across the Sna_____
when a _____
pr_____
a_____
ab_____
riv_____ into the
can____ ____ake a nose-down
crash landing on a rocky bank
at the river's edge.

Mr. Knievel was pulled un-

them _____
n_____
blu_____
pea_____
co_____
side_____
cras_____
rim_____

Bu_____
a bo_____
twice_____
of w_____

_____ e air
e and
ap-
who
g in-
night,
the

onto
aced
foot

Evel Soared To Highest Pay

TWIN FALLS, Idaho —
Evel Knievel earned $200,000
for every second of his estimated half-minute flight to
the bottom of Snake River
Canyon.

The guaranteed $6-million
payoff made him the highest
paid daredevil in history.

Knievel did not have to
complete the jump across the
quarter-mile gorge to earn
the money — just the attempt
was enough.

---

*Several young women strip-
ped to the waist. One took off
all her clothes, and, urged on
by the crowd, began performing lewd sex acts on young
men.*

Christo Javacheff created "Valley Curtain" across Rifle Gap in Colorado only to have it torn to shreds one day later in August, 1972. This project cost $700,000. Javacheff had previously wrapped part of the Australian coast line in plastic. Bumper to bumper traffic jammed the highway.

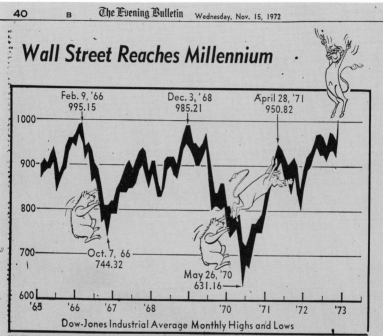

Wall Street Reaches Millennium

Feb. 9, '66
995.15

Dec. 3, '68
985.21

April 28, '71
950.82

1000

900

800

700 — Oct. 7, 66 —
744.32

May 26, '70
631.16 →

600

'65   '66   '67   '68   '70   '71   '72   '73

Dow-Jones Industrial Average Monthly Highs and Lows

OVER THE TOP—The Dow-Jones industrial average, Wall Street's traditional measure of the stock market, ended yesterday at an all-time closing high of 1,003.16, the first time it ever ended above 1,000. This tops the previous closing high of 997.07 Monday. To be sure, the index had been above 1,000 during several sessions in '66, and twice this month, but never closed above that mark. The more-widely-based Standard & Poor's general average of 500 stocks has hit closing highs frequently since 1966.

"...I will pull down my barns, and build greater; and there will I bestow all my fruits and my goods...But God said unto him, Thou fool, this night thy soul shall be required of thee...."
     Luke 12:18,20

56

The New York World Trade Center is the tallest (110 stories) and the costliest ($700 million) and the most spacious (9 million square feet) office complex on earth. It houses 50,000 employees and 80,000 visitors daily. Competing with this is Chicago's Sears Tower.

Already we have allowed 200 giant corporations to engage in mergers that control our economy. They produce over two-thirds of the products we depend on in our daily lives. Their overwhelming economic power translates into political power. These same corporations operate worldwide with 100 other corporations abroad. By 1985, these 300 corporations will control world economy.

Even the dog houses are in need of bigger barns. Meanwhile 55 million dogs and cats eat 3 million tons of food every year. Some 31 million families now own pets which zoom pet food sales to over $1.5 billion annually.

And in September, 1971, 40,000 dairy farmers sat down to a banquet in Chicago that cost about $5 million...not including tips!

All this is going on—while around the world 10 million people are dying of starvation every year!

To make sure we drink at Christmas...one major distillery spends $10 million in advertising during this season to convince us to purchase their bottled whiskey. For one of their brands, they spend over $1 million just on their Christmas box that holds the whiskey bottle!

Airlines, too, vying for more business, are buying bigger and bigger planes. The Concorde Jet will cost over $32 million! Just on one day in July or August between 4 p.m. and 8 p.m., 55 Boeing 747 jet airplanes land at the J. F. Kennedy International Airport in New York. Alighting from these planes are 20,000 passengers!

More and more wives are leaving their home to work. One-fourth of all wives with children under 3 are working. One-third of those with children under 5 are working. And one-half the mothers of school age children are working.

I PREDICT by 1977

Marijuana will be legalized and sold through cigarette companies.
Bread will be $1 a loaf. Milk will be $1 a quart.

In September, 1971 dairy farmers sat down to what was billed as "the largest feed ever held under one roof" for a dinner that cost $5 million... not including tip. Total number fed was 40,000.

BUSINESS Invites Government CONTROL

Inflation is running unchecked and is bringing America to the brink of catastrophe. Look at this:

A $20 bag of groceries of 1973 will cost $114.87 in the supermarket of 2000!

A $3000 standard automobile of today will cost $17,230.35 in the year 2000!

A $25,600 home of today will cost $147,032 in the year 2000!

These figures were recently revealed by the United States Saving and Loan League. They further warned that an American earning $10,000 in 1973 will have to earn $57,435 in the year 2000 to maintain a comparable standard of living!

AND LOOK AT THIS...

In 1970, the various divisions of Joseph E. Seagram & Sons, Inc. spent more than $6 million in advertising to back up their brands of liquor. Plus an additional $3 million was ticketed for sales promotion...and ALL OF THIS SPENT at the Christmas season! The Calvert Distillers Company division of Seagrams spent $1,600,000 on advertising at Christmas and $575,000 on sales promotion. Calvert spent more than $1 million just on Christmas packaging!

EXPENSIVE WATER...

In New York City a department store was selling **Fresh Mineral Water Spray** for $5 for an 11-ounce aerosol can. This same mineral water can be purchased for 75¢ a gallon. But if you take water...package it attractively...you can sell 11 ounces for $5!

THE PUBLIC is continuing to be fooled. If they can be fooled this easily on whiskey and water...think how much easier it will be for Antichrist to fool the populace into believing he can resolve the world's problems and bring peace! You say it can't happen here? Watch current events. You can already see the links forming that will usher in this period of Tribulation.

The Philadelphia Inquirer

Oldest Daily Newspaper in the United States—Founded 1771

Full Weather Report, 13-E

Vol. 29, No. 46

Sunday, April 7, 1974

15 CENTS

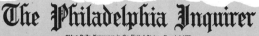

U. S. Plane Flies Atlantic In One Hour 56 Minutes

United Press International

LONDON — Moving faster than a bullet, an Air Force SR71 spy plane flew from New York to London Sunday in one hour 56 minutes, setting an unofficial speed record for the 3,490-mile Atlantic crossing, an Air Force spokesman said.

The flight cut nearly three hours off the existing record held by a British Royal Navy F4 Phantom fighter, which made the flight in 4 hours 46 minutes in 1969, the spokesman said.

The plane's two-man crew was identified as Maj. James V. Sullivan, 37, of Wheeler, Mont., and Maj. Noel F. Widdifield, 33, of Anderson, Ind.

President Ford talked by telephone with the two pilots shortly after they landed at Farnborough, England.

It was "a great flight and a magnificent accomplishment for the United States and the Air Force," the President told them.

The record-breaking flight landed at Farnborough Airfield south of London. Commenting on the transatlantic flight record, the Air Force said the SR71 flew at more than 15 statute miles above the earth, at an average speed of 1,817 MPH.

JAMES V. SULLIVAN
...record flight

NOEL F. WIDDIFIELD
...praised

This is the age of speed. This $32 million supersonic jet will be able to cross the Atlantic in a little over 3 hours (747's take 7½ hours). The new Dallas-Fort Worth airport, built at a cost of $700 million, will eventually have 234 departing gates — enough to handle over 60 million passengers a year! In the U.S. alone, by 1980 some 485 million passengers will travel the air routes annually. Land near Chicago's O'Hare airport goes for $125,000 an acre! We are entering an age of more speed...more leisure time. It will bring with it complex physical and mental problems as "bigger barns" become bigger headaches.

60

Then They Rest for Three Days

The Four-Day Work Week Gains New Ground

THE NEW YORK TIMES, SUNDAY, FEBRUARY 13, 1972

Tobacco Sales Rise Sharply Despite the Ban on TV Commercials

Now playing the Pa. Lottery is as easy as ABC!

Rizzo Has Visions Of Daily Lottery

City-operated lotteries may be in Philadelphia's future Mayor Frank Rizzo said Monday that present weekly ···not good enough because people

'Thank God It's June'

Unlikely as It Sounds, A 6-Month 'Work Year' Is Called a Possibility

More Job-Schedule Flexibility Is Urged to Expand Leisure; On River, It's 30-On, 30-Off

Just More Dull Free Time?

A WALL STREET JOURNAL *News Roundup*
The four-day week, it seems, is here to stay. So now are you ready for the six-month year? Arlin Austin is, Mr ···

THE BIGGEST MULTINATIONALS

By one definition, a multinational company is one with sales above $100 million, operations in at least six countries and overseas subsidiaries accounting for at least 20 per cent of its assets. Some 4,000 companies qualify, accounting for 15 per cent of the gross world product. The twenty biggest:

Company	Base	World Sales*	Company	Base	World Sales*
General Motors	U.S.	$28.3	ITT	U.S.	$7.3
Exxon	U.S.	18.7	Gulf Oil	U.S.	5.9
Ford Motor	U.S.	16.4	British Petroleum	Britain	5.2
Royal Dutch/Shell	Britain-Netherlands	12.7	Philips	Netherlands	5.2
General Electric	U.S.	9.4	Volkswagen	Germany	5.0
IBM	U.S.	8.3	Westinghouse Electric	U.S.	4.6
Mobil Oil	U.S.	8.2	Du Pont	U.S.	3.8
Chrysler	U.S.	8.0	Siemens	Germany	3.8
Texaco	U.S.	7.5	Imperial Chemical	Britain	3.7
Unilever	Britain-Netherlands	7.5	RCA	U.S.	3.7

*In BILLIONS

Courtesy Newsweek

Of the 20 biggest multinational companies it is interesting to note that 13 have their base in the United States. It is also of prophetic significance that all the 20 biggest are based in what may one day become the United States of Europe. Quite possibly such companies could come under the control of Antichrist during the Tribulation Period. One can imagine the power that this one man can then wield.

DO YOU KNOW WHAT YOU'RE EATING?

How much attention are you paying to what you are eating? Do you realize that right now chances are you are eating more artificial food than real food?

I've started an interesting practice lately. I've begun to read the ingredients on the packages and cans of groceries. And I've made an interesting discovery. The discovery is this: There appears to be more chemical additives than food in many of our everyday food purchases.

Is it no wonder that health spending has tripled in the last five years!

Let's take just one product...WHIPPED TOPPING. At first glance many housewives would mistake whipped topping for whipped *cream*. The difference, however, is that whipped cream is made from cream.

Here's what one whipped topping contains:

1. Hydrogenated Vegetable oil, sugar
2. Propylene Glycol Monostearate
3. Sodium Caseinate, flavoring
4. Potassium Phosphate
5. Salt
6. Polysorbate 60
7. Monoglycerides
8. Sorbitan Monostearate
9. Lecithin
10. Cellulose Gum

PLUS carob bean gum, carrageenan, artificial coloring with nitrous oxide, carbon dioxide and chloropentafluoroethane used as propellents.

In these Last Days look for more artificial food to sneak its way onto the market. By the way, what are you having for supper? Take time to read the can. You may be in for a surprise!

The Sunday Bulletin

INDEPENDENT—LOCALLY OWNED   WITH DAILY EVENING EDITION

SUNDAY, OCTOBER 7, 1973

'All-Out War' Erupts in Mideast

The Philadelphia Inquirer

Oldest Daily Newspaper in the United States—Founded 1771

WEDNESDAY MORNING, OCTOBER 10, 1973   FINAL CITY EDITION

Israeli Troops Pull Back in Sinai; Egyptians Claim Key Victories

"For God's sake, tell your people in Palestine they shouldn't proclaim a Jewish state. If they proclaim a Jewish state, within 10 days or a maximum of 15 days not a single Jew will remain alive...."

General George Marshall to Ben Gurion

General Marshall's fears proved to be unfounded...even though at the time he spoke there were only 650,000 Jews in Israel surrounded by 30 million Arabs. The year 1948 was a turning point in prophetic history. In that year the state of Israel officially came into existence.

Many Old Testament Scriptures point to this return...Isaiah 61:4, Amos 9:14, Zephaniah 2:7. In Ezekiel 36:33-38 are included the following: "I will also cause you to dwell in the cities, and the wastes shall be builded...the waste and desolate and ruined cities are become fenced, and are inhabited...so shall the waste cities be filled with flocks of men." Someday, perhaps soon, God will fulfill His ancient promises, and regather *all Israel* from the four corners of the earth (Jeremiah 23:5-8).

The missing pieces of prophecy, like a giant jigsaw puzzle, are rapidly coming together.

Israel, including its conquered territories, is 35,000 square miles (Israel proper is 8000 square miles). In its land there will soon be 3 million Jews. It has a defense budget of $1½ billion (about 22% of its total budget). By comparison defense spending accounts for only 9% of the U.S. budget; about 8% of the Soviet Union's.

Men serve 36 months active duty, remain in the reserves until age 55. Women serve 20 months of active duty.

To insure Israel's financial stability, the United Jewish Appeal in America raises close to $500 million annually. Very shortly the number of tourists visiting Israel each year will climb to the one million mark. The average tourist spends over $275 during his stay in Israel. Almost 40% of the tourists are Protestants anxious to witness with their own eyes the fulfillment of Bible prophecy.

In July, 1972 Israel formally locked into a global satellite communications system. The dedication of their new earth station was near the spot where David slew Goliath.

Teddy Kollek, mayor of Jerusalem, said: "The Jews have prayed for Jerusalem for 2000 years." And the Israel Army's chief rabbi, only hours after their paratrooopers burst into the old city of Jerusalem in June 1967, said, with tears streaming down his face: "We have come home, never to be moved again—never!"

I PREDICT by 1982

8500 Israeli's will die annually in road accidents.
Terrorists will explode a nuclear bomb.

Definite plans will at last be made to rebuild the Temple in Jerusalem. The restoration of the Temple must yet someday come to pass so that the scene may finally be set for the Antichrist to enter the world's stage. See 2 Thessalonians 2:3, 4. The Antichrist shall be an enemy both of God and of Israel.

This photograph from the Mt. of Olives was taken by the author early one fall morning. In the foreground in the shadows are graves of Jews. The sun breaks through on the inner city of Jerusalem. The Golden Gate is to the right. In a sense this unusual photograph is prophetic depicting the shadows of tragedy yet to befall the nation of Israel and the glorious sunlight of future redemption.

JERUSALEM...the "LOST" City?

Within 5 years Jerusalem, as we now know it, may become a lost city.

Two years ago Jerusalem's Mayor Teddy Kollek invited 30 foreign members of the Jerusalem Committee for Beautification to study the Master Plan for Jerusalem.

This Master Plan is in its final stage.

They met for 3 days and suggested the Master Plan be scrapped!

As you are reading this page...already 2600 housing units are being built and long range plans call for the construction of a total of 25,000 units which will house 100,000 persons.

One of the architects invited to the Jerusalem conference suggested in a written report that Jerusalem be granted extra-territorial status so that it could become a "world city" rather than a national capital.

The Talmud defines the boundaries of Jerusalem's sanctity as those areas from which one could see the Temple as one approached without it being lost to sight subsequently by a changed skyline.

Mr. Kollek's plans and that of many on the planning committee is to make Jerusalem "the New Jerusalem"...the city between earth and sky.

With the building program already in full swing...and with grandiose plans being drawn up for a Jerusalem complex of housing...one can see how in the next five years Jerusalem as we know it will become a Lost City.

Architects from all over the world converged on Jerusalem for initial planning in changing this city. And while they do not all agree on exactly what structures, what highways, and what changes should be made...they do have one thought in common...that of making Jerusalem the model city of the world.

How closely this planning ties in with events of the End Times! Could it be possible that Jerusalem itself may become the major city of the world in the Last Days? Will it become so commercialized that the Jewish people in order to combat such a trend will double their efforts to build the Temple?

Time will tell. This we do know. The face of Jerusalem is changing. And its changes are in keeping with the prophecies in Revelation. Watch for further developments in Jerusalem. They will certainly be a barometer of the end times!

MISSIONARIES FACE HARASSMENT IN ISRAEL

News clipping is from the March 17, 1972 issue of THE JERUSALEM POST.

Photo shows Mrs. Sarah Ostrovsky who is manager of the Hebrew Christian bookshop in Jaffa. She is attempting to evict one of the Jewish Defense League members who demonstrated on the premises.

Jewish Defense League members announced that they would continue to "harass" missionaries throughout Israel.

The American Board of Mission to the Jews has also witnessed pressure exerted on their ministry. On Friday, April 2nd, 1971 they planned to televise an hour-long film titled "The Passover." The Synagogue Council of America and the New York Board of Rabbis protested and as a result several television stations refused to sell them program time. Complaints also were issued concerning the American Board's newspaper ad picturing Hebrew Christians.

Will the day of missionary activity in Israel soon come to an end?

J.D.L. PROTEST AGAINST JAFFA 'MISSIONARIES'

The Jewish Defence League's Israel branch has launched a campaign against missionary activity. According to "Yediot Aharonot" reporter Noah Klieger, J.D.L. members, led by their secretary Yosef Schneider, staged a demonstration on Wednesday evening at a bookstore run by the "Hebrew Christians," 42 Rehov Yefet in Jaffa. The shop is managed by Mrs. Sarah Ostrovsky.

The J.D.L. claimed that the "Hebrew Christians" are trying to proselytize immigrants who are staying at a Jewish Agency hostel located in the same building.

After sticking posters on the shop window proclaiming "These are Missionaries," the demonstrators entered the shop, which contains religious literature in many languages, including Russian, English and Spanish. They demanded that Mrs. Ostrovsky cease her "missionary activities." Speaking fluent Hebrew, Mrs. Ostrovsky vehemently denied the charges and tried to evict the young men from her shop.

Finally she called the police, who requested her and three of the demonstrators to go down to headquarters to give evidence.

J.D.L. members announced that they would continue to "harass" missionaries throughout the country.

THE DAY for MISSIONARIES in ISRAEL has just about ENDED!

Shocked?

You shouldn't be!

Most Christians (**not all**...but most) are so concerned about acquiring their own personal needs and luxuries...a second car, a second home, money in the bank...stocks, bonds...a local church building program...that they have completely forgotten what the Christian message is all about.

It's one of Satan's deceptive detours...get the Christian so involved in his own personal life...so involved in so-called Christian "activities" such as committees, church socials, church athletics, tea parties and in further saturating the already over-evangelized...that no time (and certainly no monetary sacrifice) can be devoted to those who for the most part have never heard the Gospel **once!**

God's chosen people - the Jew - (with the exception of a handful of missionaries) is perhaps the most neglected group with respect to the opportunity to hear the Gospel of salvation.

AND LOOK AT THE NEWS CLIPPING TO THE LEFT!

What few missionaries there are in Israel soon face extinction. I PREDICT that by 1975 **no missionaries** will be allowed in Israel!

I PREDICT here's how it will come about: **First** as the article in The JERUSALEM POST reveals...The Jewish Defense League and orthodox Jews will start brush fires of agitation blaming the missionary for the growing unrest in Israel. **Second,** by 1974 the United States will open their embassy in JERUSALEM. This will be a forerunner of the United States of Europe setting up a headquarters in JERUSALEM...where Anti-christ will finally take dictatorial control and desecrate the Temple (Daniel 9:27; 2 Thessalonians 2:3-4).

With unrest building, and hostility increasing against the missionary... the United States will ask (order!) all U.S. missionaries to leave the country "in the interest of peace and harmony." This, I PREDICT!

Israeli soldiers on guard for new war in Middle East take part in special desert maneuvers with armored tank division.

FIRING PIN ON ISRAEL NOW SET....

This headline appeared recently and most people overlooked it...
CHINA RECOGNIZED BY TURKEY.

Turkey no longer recognizes Free China stating that "the People's Republic of China is the sole legal government of China." Turkey will now allow Chinese communist aircraft to use Turkish airports. LOOK AT YOUR MAP! Turkey was the **only** land area that blocked Russia from Israel! And, Turkey is one of our NATO allies! With Turkey hosting Chinese communist aircraft, Canada selling wheat to Red China, and the U.S. President drinking toasts in China with mass murderers, can we not wonder if the free world really possesses the moral fiber necessary to stop communism from taking the world?

71

ISRAEL COMBATING WAVE OF STRIKES

Labor Problem Is One of Several Internal Issues

Juvenile Crime Rises in Israel; Police Blame Growing Drug Use

By CLAUDE LEWIS
Of The Bulletin Staff

Jerusalem — Crime by juveniles is rising significantly throughout Israel. Though it is denied officially, a good deal of it has been traced to the widening use of narcotics.

Shopkeepers in Jerusalem and Tel Aviv express concern about the increase in robberies of shops, gas stations and other small businesses.

"There was a time when I didn't think ......

learning these tricks in the Army," he said. "They bring home souvenirs and, before you know it, they're sticking them in somebody's face."

Police Reluctant

Most policemen are either reluctant to discuss the problem or will admit only to a slight increase. However, Inspector Slomo Gal, of the Juvenile division, readily acknowledges that crime is up among juveniles and offers a few examples.

In 1969, about 11,000 ...

have been cases of pocketbook snatching, mugging and holdups. Very few persons have been shot or stabbed, although street assaults have occurred. Women still are unafraid to walk on the streets at night.

According to Jerusalem's mayor, Teddy Kollek, there were a total of four murders in his city last year.

Inspector Gal said:

"Most of that we have to deal with so far as juveniles are concerned is shoplifting...

A Jerusalem policeman grappling with an Israeli activist during 1971 riots. One bystander watching windows being broken cried, "My God, is this now happening here? I've read about all these things in American cities, but this is Jerusalem and this is Israel."

72

JERUSALEM in JEOPARDY

Recent events indicate a "pattern of problems" which may soon engulf JERUSALEM in bitter conflict.

Jerusalem has opened up its first sex boutique, *Eros*.

Others have opened up in Tel Aviv.

The culture of drugs has now infiltrated Israel.

What Israelis once considered a city of promise, is now a city of problems.

Jerusalem has changed overnight. From a small, Bible-like-days town before the Six Day War...it has now sprouted to a population which soars above 300,000.

There has been a great rush to rebuild the city without much regard for the economic and social consequences.

The poor in Jerusalem make up for more than 16% of its population. Almost 40% of the population receive help from the Welfare Department. Over 22,000 children in Jerusalem are in need of help from the city welfare.

The number of teenage girls involved in prostitution in Jerusalem has increased dramatically since before the Six Day War. Jerusalem has suddenly become a booming tourist town and young girls from large, low income, over-crowded homes can earn quick money through prostitution.

In spite of this, Jerusalem's welfare budget is less, in real terms, than last year's budget although costs have risen 15-20%.

You can look for the face of Jerusalem to change. Don't be surprised if the Valley of Hinnom (Potter's Field) soon becomes a 6 lane highway. Camels, donkeys and sheep will disappear. Jerusalem will become a cosmopolitan city with night clubs, theatres and thousands of cars daily inundating its environs. Its crystal-clear skyline will soon be a smog-filled valley...where one can only observe the Dome of the Rock on brisk, windy days.

Look for many governments, including the United States, to switch their embassies from Tel Aviv to Jerusalem. Another indication of the last days! (Read Zechariah 12:9 to see the importance of Jerusalem in the end-times).

Architect's suggestion for a north-south highway through the Valley of Hinnom in Jerusalem would significantly change skyline.

Photograph is not blurred. This aerial view shows cloud of smoke that pours from quarry that already is polluting the air over Jerusalem.

A resident of the Sea of Galilee, frustrated with taxes and scarcity of parts for his Henry J, cut away the engine section and replaced it with a horse.

Israelis are grateful and understandably proud to be back once again in the land of their Temple. They willingly make sacrifices. Coffee is $2.50 a pound. An ordinary Dodge car costs $15,000. A compact car, $7500. Israel is growing. In 1972, over 25,000 Jewish couples married.

Israel is also now becoming a producer and exporter. Jerusalem exports over 30 million flowers annually, mostly to Europe. Diamonds are Israel's greatest export. In more technical items, just 30 miles from Jerusalem—for example—is one of the most advanced aircraft industries in the world. It employs over 12,000 people who have come from 80 different countries...and who speak some 40 different languages.

Meanwhile the Housing Ministry has a plan of its own. Its plan is to develop an enormous residential area for 50,000 persons on the empty Judean hills. Look at the photograph to the left. If it seems hazy to you, IT IS! The haze is created by a cloud of smoke you can see every day that comes from the quarry where stone is gathered to complete this building plan. This has added immensely to the pollution over the Jerusalem valley.

THIS WAS PALESTINE

The words "Palestine" and "Palestinian" are often in the Middle East news these days. Here, briefly, is their meaning:

Palestine, the area that was long under Turkish rule...then under British mandate before Israel was created in 1948...no longer exists as an entity. In general, it means Holy Land.

The word PALESTINE comes from the Greek for Philistia, home of the ancient Philistines.

The area has been split between Israel and Jordan since 1948.

Palestinians in general are the Arabs who lived in Palestine under the British mandate, or those who are descended from these people.

About 800,000 of these left when Israel was created or fled during the Arab-Israeli war that began then. Many of them and their descendants still occupy refugee camps, mostly in Jordan or the Gaza Strip along the Mediterranean.

Hundreds of thousands of Arabs live *wretchedly* in refugee camps. Most everywhere, even children carry *weapons*. An Arab woman explained, "The gun is our only way to reach our homeland."

Many people think because the Jews are returning to Israel that there is a resurgence towards the things of God. This is furthermost from the truth. Only 15% of the Jews in Israel are active religiously. And it will not be until the Tribulation Period that the Jewish people will turn to Christ in large numbers.

The Middle East is a place of wonder but it is also the sight of future conflicts.

From a moral standpoint, people are divided over who actually owns the land.

> The land that is now the modern state of Israel was populated mostly by Arabs and other non-Jews for most of the time between A.D. 70 and the early years of the 20th Century. The conflict that has arisen is because the Jewish people have also considered this land their own for 4000 years and today the existence of the state of Israel is a 25-year-old fact.

> The Arabs believe that some sort of statue of limitations should apply. That the Hebrews lived in Palestine for 2000 years before Christ should not entitle them to a perpetual title to part of it, any more than the American Indians are entitled to a perpetual title to North America. Territories have changed hands through all of history, and there is no such thing as an eternal lease.

The above was the observation made in a special report made by The National Observer recently.

The Israelis see it otherwise. In their opinion, the land that is now Israel has always been Israel—at least since Abraham and his kinsmen moved there from what is now Iraq 4000 years ago.

For centuries the idea of a Jewish national home has been part of the Jewish consciousness and the awful persecution of European Jews by Hitler brought this desire to a climax. Thus we have what perhaps is the crux of the Arab-Israeli dispute.

An armed Arab cavalry charges across the plains.

Israeli soldiers on horses regroup for attack. Horses could play a major role when Russia invades Israel and in the battle of Armageddon.

Arab refugees await processing near Allenby Bridge in Israel. The wire
fence is symbolic of the division of Arab and Jew which one day will erupt
into worldwide conflict.

Black September Commandos: Elusive Trail in Six Countries

Continued From Page 1, Col. 2

Arab commandos, which has failed to shake Israel with its conventional guerrilla tactics—

ultramilitants from the Fatah's ranks.

But the view of Western intelligence men and Israeli and Jordanian officials put forw—

The Evening Bulletin

Arab Grenade Kills All Israeli Hostages; Deaths Total 17 but Olympics Continue

'No Teachers, No School,' Costanzo Says

3 Guerillas Held; 5 Die In Ambush

Skyjackers Force Release Of 3 Olympic Terrorists

No Signing On Tuesday, Agnew Says

Hostages 'Safe' in Tripoli

BELGRADE, Yugoslavia—Two Palestinian guerilla...

Jordan and Israel Hated

Black September hates Jordan because King Hussein's Army crushed the Arab commando movement in that country in a campaign that began in September, 1970—an event that is the origin of the group's name. It hates Israel because it says the Israelis have usurped the Palestinian homeland.

Black September also showed fallibility last month, the Jordanians say, when it mailed four letter-bombs from Amsterdam to high Jordanian officials in Amman.

At any rate, when the letters were intercepted at Amman's main post office, they were found to contain crudely printed Black September cards that seemed intended not for Jordanians but for Israelis.

The cards, according to an official, said in Arabic and in slightly misspelled English: "Because you have usurped our

Terrorists Slay 22 at Tel Aviv Airport

TEL AVIV (UPI)—Three neatly dressed Japanese men who had just arrived at Lod International Airport aboard a flight from Rome pulled guns and hand grenades out of their luggage last night and opened fire on about 300 persons in the arrival lounge.

In Beirut, the militant Arab guerilla Popular Front for the Liberation of Palestine claimed the three were members of that organization.

IN TOKYO, the Japanese Foreign Office identified the survivors, of Osaka, and the two dead men as 77, 70, Yamaguchi.

One of the gunmen raced out to the edge of the runway and opened up on an El Al plane arriving from London, splattering it with bullet holes, then threw a grenade at a parked Scanair charter jet waiting to load its passengers, mostly Christian pilgrims from Scandinavia.

An airport employe, Jean Claude Zeitoun, saw the man on the runway, watched him throw down his

Israeli soldiers watch as a mother mourns loss of her son.

82

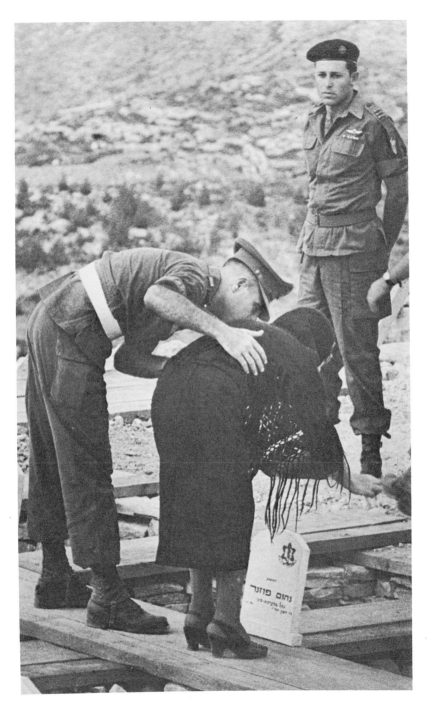

Paper peace symbols were pinned to mortarboards at Vassar at recent graduation ceremony.

At the "...time of the end: many shall run to and fro, and knowledge shall be increased."

Daniel 12:4

One of the significant trends of our age is the rapid acceleration of knowledge.

But 2 Timothy 3:7 is a clear picture of today's educational demise, for it accurately depicts this age as "Ever learning, and never able to come to the knowledge of the truth."

In India, students recently sought the right to cheat on their annual university exams! They became so violent in their protest, they killed one teacher.

Hard times are here for thousands of scientists and engineers with premium educations. No longer is the Ph.D. degree an automatic passport to a well-paid job. There are approximately 45,000 unemployed scientists and engineers. It is estimated that in 1975-1979 over 200,000 additional Doctorates will be awarded!

Some Universities are giving degrees in Magic and Occult. Human sexuality classes are springing up on many college campuses, complete with explicit movies.

Meanwhile the cost of public school education rises. The approximately 46 million students cost some $45 billion annually to educate. The new trend is the "no-mark" grading system where students are automatically passed just to get them up into the next grade. Despite such new permissive methods...many still are graduating from high school who cannot properly read or write!

It's even becoming dangerous in some areas to go to school. Some city high schools require as many as 150 safety guards patrolling the vicinity. Schools report a jump upward in assaults on teachers by students. Over 1500 incidents were recorded recently in Philadelphia in one year. And...the number of unreported incidents could easily double this figure!

Vandalism in New York City's schools runs about $4 million a year! Over $1 million of this was for broken windows!

To economize, many school systems are laying off teachers.

One educator has suggested that the only answer is to "nationalize the big-city school systems..." and let the Federal government take them over (with their problems and deficits).

I PREDICT by 1980

Many big-city school systems will end their year in April. The average college tuition and living cost will zoom to $8000 a year.

Two-year high schools will be seriously considered.

Parochial schools will be receiving federal aid. This will be done (1) to save them from bankruptcy, and (2) to save the public schools from a flood tide of students (if the parochial schools closed down) that would inundate the already overcrowded and near-bankrupt public educational systems.

Young people protesting at Capitol building.

STRIKE PERIL HALTS SCHOOL BOND SALE

There's an old song which goes something like this: "You'll never miss the water till the well runs dry." This article on school strikes has a somber prophetic implication. In your days of school, do you ever recall a strike that threatened to close the schools?

What is happening? The population is exploding. Schools are overcrowded. Millions of dollars are being spent by schools to repair vandalism. Student revolts are placing students in control of much of education. School principals are afraid to establish dress codes. Teachers are striking for more pay, less hours. Many teachers fear for their life in their classes.

What will happen? In the next few years, many schools may simply fail to open. Not enough money. No teachers. Only the privileged will be able to go to school. Some schools may even be turned into housing units. Others will be running questionable sessions directed by radical elements. This near chaos will be one of the main reasons Americans may yet welcome a dictatorship government.

Right now, every year brings us closer to such governmental control!

Eighth-Grade Student Arrested
In Slaying of Teacher at Leeds

By DON HASH

In February, 1971 at least 20 school teachers were beaten by a group of youths in Newark, New Jersey. The youths were armed with clubs and lengths of pipe. The teachers were on strike.

WHAT DOES THE FUTURE HOLD for EDUCATION?

I PREDICT that by the year 2000...

Students will not go to school. They will learn through TV receivers built into their heads. These sensing devices on the same wave lengths as computers will enable a student to learn enormously faster than at present.

Teachers, school systems, diplomas and degrees will cease to exist. Learning centers sponsored by industry will replace the present system.

It will become illegal to require a certain degree in order to qualify for a particular job.

MAN INTO SUPERMAN
The Promise and Peril of the New Genetics

ARTIST ERNST TROVA'S "WALKING MAN"
A peer with dark forces.

TIME, APRIL 19, 1971

"We must create a future man with greater personal freedom and originality — a member of a psychocivilized society, happier, less destructive and better balanced than present man."

Neurophysiologist, School of Medicine, Yale

90

The late author, C. S. Lewis, warned more than a quarter century ago that "man's power over Nature is really the power of some men over other men, with Nature as their instrument."

We have advanced into an era of "dangerous knowledge"—knowledge that accumulates faster than the wisdom of man to manage it.

Electrode implants in chimpanzees are now being used experimentally to control the actions of the animal by computer. Very shortly these experiments will be conducted on human beings in the name of science. In the future the use of such dangerous knowledge can be used by a tyrannical leader to create "push-button" people.

Electrodes are now being implanted into the brains of rats to locate specific "pleasure centers."

Scientists are seriously studying the idea that super-geniuses will some day be produced either by increasing brain size or through genetic manipulation. Another prospect is to transplant brain cells to newborn infants or to the fetus in the womb so that babies will be born with rote knowledge—language skills, multiplication tables and shared consciousness.

Man, say the scientists, could one day clone (asexually reproduce himself) creating thousands of virtually identical twins from a test tube full of cells carried through gestation by donor mothers or hatched in an articial womb. Cloning would make it possible to develop a passive community or an aggressive community, depending on the whim of the scientist.

One prominent psychologist, at the annual meeting of American Psychological Association in September, 1971, suggested that mind-affecting drugs should be developed to prevent political leaders from using their power in inhumane and unethical ways. He further recommended that world leaders should be required to take this medication to subdue their propensity for violence.

Already American drug companies produce some 8 billion pills yearly or 40 for every man, woman and child in this country...many of which exercise some form of mind control.

There is another unseen physical force in our world that also can accomplish an amazing range of things upon the mind. It has the ability to control mind action and kill. This force is sound. Scientists are finding new ways to use this energy. It is already possible to use this force destructively!

I PREDICT by 1981

A human being — born of clonal or laboratory reproduction — will appear on this earth.

Pleasure consoles to stimulate pleasure centers will be in the experimental stage, ready for marketing by 1985.

Rhesus monkey receiving electrical stimulus in the hypothalamus to induce aggressive behavior. Photograph was taken in research laboratory in Atlanta, Georgia.

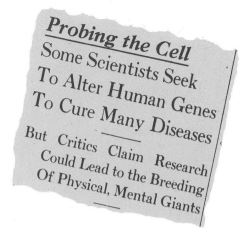

DRUGS ARE FOUND TO MAKE RATS KILL

Chemicals Applied to Brain Seem to Control Urge

Special to The New York Times

PRINCETON, N. J., Feb. 14—A team of psychologists at Princeton University has located an apparent "killing control" site in the brain of the rat and identified brain chemicals that elicit and suppress the tendency to kill when applied to the area.

Probing the Cell
Some Scientists Seek To Alter Human Genes To Cure Many Diseases
But Critics Claim Research Could Lead to the Breeding Of Physical, Mental Giants

TERRIFYING CONTROL DEVICES D/E/V/E/L/O/P/E/D

While American Christians slumber into their "attend church every Sunday" routine little do they realize that soon they will be in for a rude awakening!

Already Government agencies are developing terrifying control devices designed to subdue large groups of people.

While these devices are supposedly being prepared to control riots and those who break the law...any Christian who is perceptive and knows prophecy...realizes that these same control devices may one day be employed in the Tribulation Period against Christians (who will be considered law breakers and unpatriotic).

There are already experiments going on to control human behavior. A specific control mechanism is a peculiar complex of flickering, steady and unseen light rays. Another device employs the use of audible sounds and other tones too high for the human ear to hear.

WHAT THEY WILL DO: The flickering light will be able to throw off the normal electric rhythms of the brain. This will lead to confusion... may even break down the brain's ability to control the body.

Inaudible sounds...which are outside the human hearing range can cause unendurable pain, cripple a person's ability to function.

Even electronic sound devices are being experimented with which, when perfected, will interupt, distort or mask speeches of individuals at meeting places.

I PREDICT these devices will be perfected and in use before 1977!!

Another hideous weapon being developed is a Giant Pulse Laser which, reportedly, can bring rabbit and monkey eyes to the boiling point, cause bleeding and an actual explosion in the eye. The laser beam... when directed on a group of individuals could cause instant blindness! The beam works fast...less than a micro-second...instant blindness! America—it is time to turn to God!

Half of '71 Deaths On U.S. Highways Linked to Alcohol

WASHINGTON, Sept. 13 (Reuters) — Almost half the 55,000 road deaths in the United States last year were attributable at least in part to alcohol, a Government report said today.

The report on road and vehicle safety said that the problem of drunken driving was more serious than many believed and that 27,000 deaths had been alcohol-related.

Abington Hospital Awarded 1st Special Liquor Permit

HARRISBURG (UPI) — The Liquor Control Board has issued the first permit for special occasion liquor sales to Abington Memorial Hospital, Montgomery County, for its annual fund raising event in June.

The LCB said a recent amendment to the state liquor code allows the issuing of special permits to hospitals, religious institutions and volunteer fire companies for liquor sales during fund raising events.

Washington Merry-Go-Round

No End Seen to Drug Fight

By JACK ANDERSON

Washington — Stopping the drug smugglers is almost a hopeless task in the opinion of the man in charge of the drug crackdown.

John Ingersoll, the nation's narcotics chief, gave congressmen a gloomy report the other day behind closed doors.

"A SPECIAL ACTION OFFICE for drug abuse prevention has been established in the White House. An office of drug abuse law enforcement has been created to attack street

"I guess, " he said, "we are going to have to resign ourselves to the fact that we are going to live with a drug problem in this country and we are going to have to cope with it the best we can."

Summarizing the problem, this lawman pointed out:

"Each year, some 210 million people come across our borders or through our ports of entry. The number of ships that call at our

---

"I've always used nudity for entertainment. That's all: entertainment. And that's what the public seems to want."

Russ Meyer, Producer of nude films

"I think of what happened to Greece and to Rome, and you see what is left...only the pillars...they became subject to the decadence that eventually destroys the civilization."

Richard Nixon, President

A few short years ago, nudity was unknown in major American films. Today it is commonplace.

A few short years ago nudity was unknown in major American magazines. Today, nudity, accompanied with explicit sordid sex scenes, is commonplace.

There are no more guidelines for nudity, according to a Motion Picture spokesman.

Sex exploitation which originated perhaps in New York and San Francisco now inundates the entire nation. Organized crime dominates much of the pornography business.

The New York police commissioner says his hands are tied. "What would have been considered pornographic only a few years ago by the courts is no longer considered so by the courts. In case after case the court has ruled in favor of the pornographic operator."

New York City has been labeled by one news magazine as "Sodom on the Hudson."

Meanwhile, sex supermarkets are a booming business in Europe. When Great Britain's first sex supermarket opened in London...within one week more than 90% of the merchandise was sold out!

Yves St. Laurent, as far back as 1968, introduced the see-through dress at a Paris fall fashion show.

One author whose books are laced with sex sells 6 million copies annually all over the world. Deferred royalties alone will give him an annual income of $500,000 from now through 1992.

Women's magazines have also latched on to this money maker. One magazine in 1972 came out with a nude man in its centerfold.

And an enterprising businessman in Minneapolis chartered a plane for passengers to spend an hour in the air on a DC-3 for lunch with a topless female entertainer.

Meanwhile, on another type of ride in Paris, tourists pay 20 cents for a 20 minute smelly ride through the sewers of Paris.

I PREDICT by 1974

Nudity will begin to appear on U.S. late evening television programs.

Pornography will appear on TV by 1980. It will be condoned by the courts.

The United States will be another Sodom and Gomorrah. Pray that 10 righteous people will remain so that God might yet spare the nation.

Nixon Warns of National Decay, Reminds Nation of Rome, Greece

By FRANK CORMIER

San Clemente, Calif. — (AP) — President Nixon says he believes the United States is approaching a period of possible decline into decadence.

But he says the news media "and perhaps even Presidents and politicians" can help matters by occasionally empha-

stopped en route here for a two-week stay.

While expressing confidence that everything will turn out right for the country, Mr. Nixon likened the United States today to ancient Greece and Rome on the eve of their declines from greatness.

"I think of what happened

maneuvering on peace in Vietnam and the Middle East.

He was accompanied to California by Richard Helms, director of the Central Intelligence Agency, just back from a secret mission to Israel and undisclosed points.

Ronald L. Ziegler, White House press secretary, said Helms gave the President and Secretary of State William P.

However, the continuing presence here of Rogers and Army Brig. Gen. Alexander Haig, Kissinger's deputy, did nothing to dispel speculation that an important foreign policy review was under way.

President Nixon's brief stop in Kansas City yesterday included a telephone call to former President Harry S. Tru-

Continued on Page 3, Column 1

Sex Exploitation Spreading Here

By MURRAY SCHUMACH

The active field of operations by prostitutes, pimps and pornography dealers has spread from the Times Square area, and now extends from Lexington to 10th Avenue and from 40th Street to the upper 50's.

Most of the sex shows, pseudo-massage and model studios and hard-core pornography movies have opened in the last few years.

A survey by The New York Times, including interviews with employes of the porno-sex business, visits to some of these place

dominates most of the pornography business, and there is strong evidence, according to Police Commissioner Patrick V. Murphy, that it has considerable control of prostitution through the pimps.

¶Businessmen and their associations are fearful that the sleazy, sometimes frightening atmosphere created by prostitution and pornography is a serious threat to the world-famous theatrical district and the restaurants and hotels that depend heavily on it.

¶There are strong indications that Supreme Court de-

tion that may make the city a forerunner in a national backlash movement reminiscent of the nineteen-twenties, when in such cities as New York and Philadelphia, all movies were shut down briefly and censorship boards sprouted.

Yet even while the pornosex business grows, some operators profess to be upset that profits are no longer as great as before, contending that this is the result of overexpansion. Their pleas of poverty are discounted by authorities in the field, but there are signs that customers may

man-days a month earlier, the Labor Department reports.

And, Now, Color Radio; You Can Color It Blue —For Plenty of Sex

• • •

Talk Ranges From Aphrodisiacs To Virginity Over Stations In Hollywood, Across the U.S.

By EARL C. GOTTSCHALK JR.
Staff Reporter of THE WALL STREET JOURNAL

HOLLYWOOD, Calif.—Today's topic on Bill Ballance's Feminine Forum on Radio Station KGBS is: "What kind of animal does your man remind you of?"

"A koala bear," says the first caller, a young woman from Long Beach. "Because he's so cute and cuddly."

"But he's be

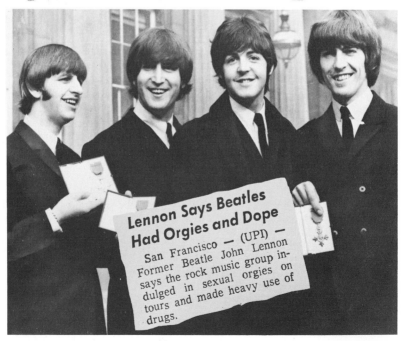

Lennon Says Beatles Had Orgies and Dope

San Francisco — (UPI) — Former Beatle John Lennon says the rock music group indulged in sexual orgies on tours and made heavy use of drugs.

This Present World...another Sodom and Gomorrah?

The moral problems that first sprouted in the European nations are now making their impact in the United States as well as in the Holy Land.

Immorality, throughout the world, now knows no bounds. Scriptures warn us in Matthew 24:12 that "because iniquity shall abound, the love of many shall grow cold." This is a sign of the last days. We are seeing a rebirth of Sodom and Gomorrah.

Even Jerusalem is showing signs of being influenced with sin and sex. Lottery tickets are sold openly outside the walls of the Old City. Jerusalem motion picture theaters show films with sexual themes and depicting rock music festivals. Nightclubs are becoming more and more evident. Even prostitution is now legal in Israel. Israeli social workers estimate that some 5000 girls under the age of 18 are engaged in this practice.

You may recall the Shakespearean phrase from your schooldays which said "There is something rotten in Denmark."

And perhaps the greatest modern avalanche of moral decay began in these Scandanavian countries with sex Fairs and flourishing sex supply stores.

In the last 2 years you have witnessed what some refer to as a "sexual revolution in the United States." Here again we see the theory of GRADUALISM take effect. First just a few barriers to moral uprightness were allowed to fall. Then as the public approved, a few more barriers were dropped. And within two years...we have witnessed a country where **anything goes!**

Coupled with this, abortion laws have been relaxed. In New York City alone more births were aborted in the last 6 months of 1970 than the number of Americans who were killed during the entire Vietnam war!

Where will it all end? God alone knows the answer! The United States need not fear that it will be overtaken by communism. Communists know that the United States, if it does fall, will fall because of decay from within.

In our age of affluence, luxury upon luxury, more money, shorter work weeks...thrills are running out. And thus many turn to the artificial mountain-top thrills of immorality and drugs, only to find suddenly a crater-filled abyss below.

Talk shows are contributing to the lax morals of our country...and unfortunately they command vast audiences...into the millions. They know sex themes build viewing audiences...and the larger the viewing audiences...the more the income from their television commercials.

Watch the late evening shows. Words that would have been taboo even a year ago are now acceptable. Hardly a show goes by on the above programs where the sex theme is not alluded to.

Wandering in the desert after their escape from Egypt, the Israelites demanded visible gods to lead them. They melted down their golden ear-rings to make a statue of a bull-calf. Has the church come full circle to again worshipping a Golden Calf of materialism and compromise?

 "The National Council of Churches envisions a potential constituency far wider than its present membership. It is hoped that Catholics and Jews may seek membership in the council."

Spokesman for the National Council at 1971 general board meeting.

Churches...Protestant, Catholic and Jewish synagogues are fast becoming big businesses. One publication has referred to them as billion dollar businesses.

Like businesses they are slowly becoming conglomerates...merging together to become more effective powers throughout the United States and throughout the world. As early as 1970, leading Catholic, Protestant and Jewish scholars met in New York to discuss areas of mutual agreement. Since then, other meetings of greater substance have been held in the Middle East and in Africa.

Churches are today more and more using their power and their funds to force social change. Representatives of 24 major religious denominations recently participated in a campaign to end the war in Vietnam.

Along with this pressure by the church...the church conglomerate was able to start and then accelerate the flow of public funds to church-related schools...breaching the historic wall between church and state. Before 1965 Federal aid was nil. Since then it is estimated to be over $500 million. Such acceptance of Federal funds places the church conglomerate in a precarious position of subservience to possible governmental control in the future. Is this a preview of the merger of Antichrist and the False Prophet (the Political Dictator with the Religious Leader — Revelation 13:11-12)?

While collectively they are merging their denominations for greater power...individually they are making the church a profitable business. It has been estimated by *"Protestants and Other Americans United for Separation of Church and State"* that the visible assets of the church (land and buildings) is at least $80 billion.

This is almost *double* the combined assets of the nation's five largest industrial corporations. Of this sum it is estimated that:

> $45 billion is held by Roman Catholics
> $28 billion by Protestants
> $7 billion by the Jewish faith

One Baptist church in Dallas has a 7 story parking and recreation building with a skating rink, gym and four bowling alleys. The National Presbyterian Center in Washington, D.C. is a $8.5 million complex with windows made up of 63,300 pieces of faceted glass.

The Mormon Church in Utah owns a newspaper, a radio-TV station, a department store and a Hawaiian tourist attraction, Laie Village. The Catholic Church has in recent years built in the Vatican a $9.6 million Papal Audience Hall and in New York City a $21 million First Avenue headquarters complex.

I PREDICT by 1979

Churches will be taxed.
There will be a merger between the National Council of Churches and the Catholic church.

"The Salvation Army Band," a hard-playing 13-member teen-age rock group, performing last month for vacationing Salvationists at the Army's Star Lake summer camp in Bloomingdale, N.J.

Salvation Army Trades Anthems for Rock Music

It's unlikely that long-haired, modly dressed members of the Salvation Army will soon be playing the Beatles' "Help" instead of "The Old Rugged Cross" on street corners across the land.

"Rock is another gimmick, but the Army itself started as a stunt—which worked," said Ray Steadman-Allen, the Head of the Army's International Music Editorial Department, headquartered in London.

The stunt was a militarily

can be interpreted by committed Christians.

In the group's opinion, Jesus is the one the Beatles are calling on in "Help" when they sing: "Help me if you can, I'm feeling down And I do appreciate your bein' 'round."

With its five singers, drums, electric organ and guitars, and a powerful brass section that got its training on street corners, the Band alternates its own arrangements of rock songs with comments on how the lyrics

60,000 teen-agers dig new hard-rock religion

The Associated Press

's on the s admit. ig it. And t up and

fish with r Harold of Glen- r of the f the Sev- Church,

gram started expanding to a nationwide basis. "We want to blanket North America with it," said a spokesman, Herbert Ford. It relies on breezy messages, aired on paid time of leading rock-music stations, offering free mailed items, produced in the same fashion.

"Jesus had a funny way of always being for people ... in helping a brother who was hurting inside," says one fan. cifully decorated issue. "He knew people were carrying around heavy things in their heads, and he wanted to liberate them ... He still does that.

"No matter how many

$21-Million First Ave. Complex To House Archdiocesan Offices

By EDWARD B. FISKE

The Roman Catholic Arch-diocese of New York announced yesterday that it would move its administrative offices from the Villard Houses, a Renaissance revival landmark on Madison Avenue, into a $215-million building to be constructed at First Avenue and 51st Street.

Church officials said that the archdiocese planned to main-

announcement and declared, "The idea of looking for a long-range tenant couldn't be more encouraging for efforts to preserve these irreplaceable buildings."

Archdiocesan officials also disclosed that two other buildings—the Cathedral Girls' High School at Lexington Avenue and 51st Street, and the Catholic Charities

Minister Urges Legal Marijuana

By LACEY FOSBURGH

Canon Walter D. Dennis Jr. of the Cathedral Church of St. John the Divine urged in a sermon yesterday that the smoking of marijuana be legalized and that the thousands of people now in jail for using it be granted immediate amnesty.

Saying that "maybe 20 million youngsters smoke marijuana regularly," the 34-year old canon told the

and irrational" ones that now stand.

"I am not advocating that we replace the traditional coffee hour after church with a turned-on smoke-in," he said, "but I am saying that if an adult comes to the coffee hour and decides to smoke marijuana instead of cigarettes, he should not be subject to criminal liability."

"Is this too much to ask

"It would be preferable to find ways toward fantasy and rapture which do not rely on chemicals and external stimulants," he continued, "just as it would be nice to induce gaiety and relaxation without martinis and bourbon, but that would require a very different society from the one we have today."

"It seems very hypocritical," he added, "for a whole population which uses pep

American Churches Are Turning to Sensitivity Training

By EDWARD B. FISKE

Sensitivity training, originated two decades ago to help industry improve its decision-making processes and give individuals deeper insight into human relations, is rapidly becoming one of the most important new elements of American church life.

Like hundreds of corporations, foundations, colleges and other secular organiza-

movement reflects the trend in society toward freer emotional expression. Many see the values inherent in sensitivity training as fundamentally religious and consider it as a fitting way to restore emotion and personal concern to congregations whose life and worship have become formal and impersonal.

The Rev. Gerald J. Judd, director of Christian Educa-

THE CHURCH IS FALLING ASLEEP...

And no-one can wake it up!

The forces of Satan have found their secret weapon. Don't fight the church. Join it. What better way is there to deteriorate the witness of the Gospel?

Satan has used two important tactics:

SUCCESS

IMITATE

SUCCESS—BY WORLDLY STANDARDS. First, make the church a successful business enterprise. Encourage large, substantial buildings (some cost over $1 million!). Bring today's standards into church constitutions by lowering them so no one will be offended. Fill the coffers of the church with money and use it for bigger buildings, bigger projects. Stuff the congregation with bigger and better everything and at the same time reduce missionary expenditures to bare minimums. Have the people so programmed that they are busy, busy, busy just about every night of the week in church activities that are self-centered.

IMITATE—WORLDLINGS DRESSED AS CHRISTIANS. With youth so fed up with the ensuing hypocrisy of the "corporation" church, encourage them to go off on another tangent. Start a multitude of Jesus Freak cults, shabbily dressed, long-haired. Give them zeal that will generate good national newspaper and magazine coverage. Pit them against the organized church. Encourage them to develop "Christian Rock," a surface Christianity that gives them a high. Then to further confuse the public, sprinkle in some honest sincere Jesus people who are showing spiritual growth. But above all...IMITATE.

In these Last Days we are witnessing many imitations..."fool's gold." As Christians we should be discerning...not susceptible to every whim of doctrine.

This could be the Church's greatest hour! But while the multitude of nations are rapidly moving across the platform of life...the church is fast asleep in the last pew. Who will wake YOUR church up? Will YOU?

THE MODERN DAY CHURCH

This illustration appeared in a secular national magazine. It is a sad commentary on many of today's churches, isn't it.

How often have you witnessed the message of the cross supplanted...pushed aside...even denied...and in its place the message of a social gospel!

What about your church? Has it diverted from its original purpose...to reach and win souls to Christ...uplift Christians? Is it a social center?

If a spiritual X-ray could be taken of your church (or of your own personal life) would the cross be a basketball net...a bowling pin...a swimming pool...the signpost of a weekly social get-together? Or a place of prayer, of dedication, of sacrifice of one's personal life...of soul winning?

Is it no wonder that in these End Times...many will seek to blame the church for the ills of the world!

103

PEKING REVIEW 46

November 17, 1972

北京周报

Soviet Proposal on Disarmament Is a Fraud

— Chiao Kuan-hua's speech at U.N. General Assembly and "Renmin Ribao" Commentator's article

The Cambodian People March On

More Works by Marx, Engels, Lenin And Stalin Published in China

Soviets still arming against nuclear war

MOSCOW (UPI). — The Soviet Union still fears the possibility of nuclear war with America and is arming against it, in spite of last month's nuclear-freeze agreements, the Communist party newspaper "Pravda" said yesterday.

"The limitation of strategic arms does not eliminate the danger of nuclear war, although it goes in this direction," "Pravda" commentators O. Grinev and V. Pavlov said in an article on U.S.-Soviet relations.

"Until this danger is liquidated, the Soviet Union has and will take all the necessary steps to guarantee its security and that of its allies.

"The Moscow (strategic arms) agreements take this into ac-

The "Pravda" article concluded optimistically by saying "a realistic point of view" now holds official sway among U.S. leaders, who have finally abandoned attempts to gain permanent military superiority.

"The Moscow agreements started off the process of limiting strategic arms, and what we should do now is to carry this process to a constructive conclusion," "Pravda" said.

Soviet-Egypt ships speeded up

MOSCOW (AP). — Soviet freighters which ply the sea route between the Black Sea port of Odessa and Egypt have started operating on an "express schedule," "Izvestia" reported Wednesday night.

"We would like to tell you in all frankness that if Israel continues its adventurism...the Soviet Union will be forced to see to it that the Arab states have means at their disposal, with the help of which a due rebuff to the arrogant aggressor could be made."

Alexei N. Kosygin
Premier, Soviet Union

Russia's rising interest in Middle East affairs is preparing the ground for an eventual all-out war on Israel. It is doubtful that the United States will interfere.

On May 22nd, 1972 President Nixon met with Soviet leaders in Moscow. The Moscow summit produced an unprecented surge of agreements. What many do not realize is that in 7 summit meetings between a U.S. President and a Soviet leader, 25 agreements have been reached. The Soviets have violated 24 of these!

America's lead in nuclear striking power has vanished over the past 10 years. Just 10 years ago the U.S. had a lead over the Russians of 8 to 1. Five years ago it was 4 to 1. Today, Russia has taken the lead in ICBM's (Intercontinental ballistic missiles).

Russia's greatest desire now, with another U.S. peace pact under her belt, is to gain access to the vast riches of the Mideast oil fields.

Up to this point the United States and other Western-controlled firms have dominated the gasoline production industry, refining and marketing oil from Arab nations for the last 50 years. Now Russia is attempting to woo the Middle East oil interests completely away from us by propaganda and arms aid. To accomplish this she is engaging in an anti-U.S. and an anti-European drive.

The Middle East contains more than 75% of the non-Communist world's oil reserves. Western Europe obtains 80% of its oil supplies from the Mideast.

Japan gets more than 90% from the same source.

One oil economist says, "There is no alternative to Middle East oil."

By controlling Middle East oil, Russia hopes to be able to drive out the American presence in that region. This will be critical, particularly when some economists calculate that the U.S. by 1980 may have to import as much as 50% of its oil from the Middle East. Is it no wonder that President Nixon after his summit with Russian leaders went out of his way to fly to Iran for a special conference!

Russia is aiming to control oil in the Middle East as part of its quest for world communist dominion. This aim has brought about Russia's desire to control the Arab nations. This quest for power has also caused Russia to make Israel's existence difficult. This is all a part of the chain of events which will yet someday see Russia invade Israel. In the Old Testament prophecies, Ezekiel 38:1-39:16 describes this war and its outcome.

I PREDICT by 1978

Russia will completely dominate Middle East oil.
Russia will break the "nuclear-freeze" agreement made with the United States in 1972.

SOVIET RECORD IN 25 SUMMIT AGREEMENTS with the UNITED STATES

HONORED:

1

BROKEN:

24

Vladimir Hall in the Kremlin, May 23, 1972. Presidents Nixon and Nikolai V. Podgorny of Russia sign peace pacts.

York Times

TUESDAY, MAY 23, 1972 — Higher newsstand price in air delivery cities M 15 CENTS

NIXON AND BREZHNEV TALK 2 HOURS
SOON AFTER PRESIDENT'S ARRIVAL;
MOSCOW WELCOME IS RESTRAINED

Bulletin
WITH SUNDAY MORNING EDITION

DAILY HOME DELIVERY 70¢ PER WEEK; WITH SUNDAY $1.05 PER WEEK

Kissinger Talking
To Soviets About
War and Trade

Meeting

The Philadelphia Inquirer

Oldest Daily Newspaper in the United States—Founded 1771

TEN CENTS   Vol. 286, No. 148   SATURDAY MORNING, MAY 27, 1972   FINAL CITY EDITION

U.S., Soviet Agree to Curb Missile Race

**Treaty Text
And Analyses
On Page 4**

Kosygin:
'A Great
Victory'
By JAMES McCARTNEY

How Superpowers Balanced Their Arsenals of Terror

Intercontinental Ballistic Missiles (ICBMs)
PRESENT STRENGTH

Evening Bulletin
WITH SUNDAY MORNING EDITION

G   WEDNESDAY, MAY 24, 1972   DAILY HOME DELIVERY 70¢ PER WEEK; WITH SUNDAY $1.05 PER WEEK

U.S. and Russia Agree
To Nuclear Arms Ceiling

President Nixon and Soviet Premier Aleksei Kosygin toast one another in the Kremlin's St. Vladimir Hall after signing agreements in May, 1972.

THE RUSSIANS and FLYING SAUCERS

While many reports of flying saucers can be explained, a careful study of the Air Force investigation will reveal that there is a 30% ratio of unexplained cases. Even the American Institute of Aeronautics and Astronautics, a society of aerospace scientists and engineers, finds it difficult to ignore some well-documented and unexplained cases which have a high degree of creditability.

For centuries scientists refused to believe in meteorites and they denied their existence. Years later they recognized their mistake.

While the Russians may not have flying saucers, they have been successful in placing a multitude of instruments in space. They have built the first experimental laboratory to orbit the earth. Could another of their inventions—or ours—be the Flying Saucer? Or is the saucer of imaginary—or of supernatural—origin?

A Soviet spy satellite was reported to have remained stationary over Israel for 14 days not long ago. It presumably transmitted to Moscow photographic images taken of the Israeli missile sites and other strategic military installations.

SOVIET-AMERICAN SPACE FLIGHT

In 1975, a Soyuz and an Apollo will rendezvous in outer space and crew members will transfer from one vehicle to the other. This Soviet-American space flight may set the stage for future persecution of Israel in the coming Tribulation Period.

RUSSIA'S GAME IN MIDEAST OIL FIELDS

Power ... prestige ... access to vast riches. Those are the prizes Moscow seeks in the Arab world. For the West, it could mean painful adjustment.

Reported from
BEIRUT, LONDON, WASHINGTON

latest Arab moves, with Russian hel
many cases, are taking place.

Involved is far more than the
of the U. S. and other Western-c
oil firms that have dominate
tion, refining and marketing
this region for the last 50

The Middle East
75 per c
world'

Kosygin Letter Favors Intervention To Force Israel Out of Arab Lands

oin the incident. One is a con
was acting.

London — (AP) — Texts of the Soviet Union," Mr. Nixon
exchanged between
Nixon

cilitate a political solution.
"We are prepared to conti

CAN RUSSIA TAKE OVER THE ARAB WORLD?

SPAIN

TURKEY

Mediterr

ISIA

THE JERUSALEM POST

Israel poisons the atmosphere: Brezhnev

A New York city policeman was on duty at the Soviet Mission to the U.N. when a woman slipped past, stood opposite the mission and cried out, pleading, "Let my people go." The policeman told her she should leave, and though she was so upset that at one point she slumped down, she wept and left.

1971 anti-war demonstrators at nation's Capitol building in Washington, D.C.

"As an American, I am shocked at the way Republican and Democrats alike are playing directly into the Communist design of 'confuse, divide and conquer.'...The President denies that we are in a revolution. There are many who would disagree with such appraisal. Anarchy may seem nearer to many of us than it really is.... Extremism...is increasingly forcing upon the American people the narrow choice between anarchy and repression."

Margaret Chase Smith
U.S. Senator, Maine

1976...the 200th birthday for the United States. Yet every day we Americans are becoming a smaller minority.

We are increasing at only 1% a year. The rest of the world increases twice as fast. By the year 2000, one person in 24 will be an American. Should this present earth last another 100 years...at that time only one in 46 will be an American.

Today already 73% of Americans live on only 1% of the nation's land area! And we are faced with 6 paradoxes:

The paradox of freedom:
> Where does freedom begin? Where does it end? In a 1971 anti-war demonstration about a half million protesters converged on Washington, D.C. More than 7000 were arrested. The price for controlling this demonstration cost the American taxpayers in excess of 4 million dollars.

The paradox of power
> Never before has so much power been placed in the hands of one man...the President of the United States. Yet at times, even his hands are tied!

The paradox of wealth
> Never before have so many Americans enjoyed so much wealth, yet unemployment and poverty cause continued internal conflict.

The paradox of speed
> Apollo 8 whizzed to the moon at a speed that would have taken it around the earth in less than an hour. Yet in many downtown areas a horse and buggy can travel faster than an automobile!

The paradox of knowledge
> 90% of all scientists who have ever lived are still alive. In 2 seconds computers do mathematical problems that would take a man 38 years to solve. Yet the nation is glutted with unemployed Ph.D.'s and knowledge alone is not resolving the bitter conflicts which the U.S. faces daily.

The paradox of communications
> Satellites parked in orbit beam news occurring around the earth the moment it happens. Yet never before has the United States government been so frustrated in its inability to communicate its messages to its many and divisive elements of the population.

Crime, poverty, unrest are the snowball that is reaching mammoth proportions. Will it drive the United States into a merger with European nations? Time will tell.

I PREDICT by 1980

Violence will force the adoption of U.S. policies which will employ stringent controls of repression. The President will have unlimited "emergency" powers.

Government will exercise control over pricing, employment, and many freedoms we now take for granted.

The Fig Leaf Has Fallen:
Movie Nudity Now Routine

By BOB THOMAS

HOLLYWOOD — (AP) — Five years ago, nudity was unknown in major American films. Today, the display of bosom and behinds is common and the trend continues toward total exposure.

wood — "the modern Sodom and Gomorrah" — that a frightened industry adopted a Production Code which now seems ludicrous in its strictness.

Among its strictures: "Complete nudity is never permitted . . . Undressing scenes

Curious Yellow" and the flood of other Scandinavian sex films. The lesson has not been wasted on American filmmakers.

The result is that more and more actresses — and actors — are being asked to play nude scenes.

Youths scuffle with an elderly woman trying to prevent her from attending the 59th annual Flower Mart in downtown Baltimore, May, 1971. While this attack was going on...hundreds stood by and watched. Such indifference could well characterize the Tribulation Period as others watch Christians being persecuted.

116

HAS THE AMERICAN DREAM become a NIGHTMARE?

The United States is at a crossroads. On the one hand are the radicals who want to burn everything down and pattern our government after Russia's so called free society.

On the other hand there are those who might be termed "right wing" who have as their battle cry: "America, love it or leave it."

Speaking in general terms...the radical causes a law and order rebound, with more stringent laws, more government control. Eventually the democratic processes of government give way to a more expedient militaristic control...generate a super sensitive spying system such as we have already seen in effect by the U.S. Army.

Those who oversimplify by stating: "America, love it or leave it" are sometimes blind to the ills facing our nation today. They, in effect, encourage a blind patriotism that also eases the way for a leader such as antichrist to take control. Undoubtedly in pre-World-War 2 days, the Germans had a similar phrase: "Germany, love it or leave it." Unfortunately the day came too soon, when in the hands of a dictatorship, they were neither able to love it or leave it.

The American Government including the Supreme Court represent a paradox today. Look at the newspaper clippings to the left and on pages 94 and 96. Both tell the fact that obscenity is now a way of life in America and is not breaking any laws.

One would think that with such laxness in the enforcement of laws concerning morality that there would be an equal laxness in other areas of government. But, quite to the contrary. **Never before in history** has the United States government exercised so much control over its people, over business, over industry! The chairman of the board of Metropolitan Life Insurance Company in his investigation of the Defense Department stated: "The Defense Department is the single, most wasteful, incompetent, overstaffed department in the Government. It consists largely of paper-shufflers and memo-writers."

Such waste and incompetence is also found in all branches of government. The United States branches of government have grown too big, too fast. The United States Government is the BIGGEST ORGANIZATION on Earth. It employs over 6.5 million people and pays them over 40 BILLION dollars a year! Would it surprise you to know that 1 out of every 13 Americans works for the United States Government?

What does this mean? It's time for Christians to stop and think and to work to make our country one that gets back to honoring God's Word.

If Supreme Court decisions allowing pornography continue...and if the Government becomes larger and stronger, it will not be long before an antichrist can walk in and take complete control without a ripple of complaint. And that day is not far away!

The Philadelphia Inquirer

Oldest Daily Newspaper in the United States—Founded 1771

Friday, August 9, 1974 — 15 CENTS

Nixon Resigns; Ford to Step Up

Successor Hails 'Great Sacrifice'

Kissinger To Stay, He Says

By JULES WITCOVER

WASHINGTON — Gerald R. Ford Jr., a 60-year-old Grand Rapids, Mich., lawyer never aspired to national office but had it thrust upon him as a result of two of the greatest political scandals in American history, will become the 38th President of the United States today.

President Forced Out By Scandal

By ROBERT S. BOYD
Inquirer Washington Bureau

WASHINGTON—Richard Milhous Nixon, the 37th President of the United States, resigned in sorrow Thursday night, the first to be torn from office by scandal in the history of the Republic.

The Philadelphia Inquirer

Oldest Daily Newspaper in the United States—Founded 1771

Monday, September 9, 1974 — 15 CENTS

Ford Grants Nixon Pardon; Press Aide Quits in Protest

By SAUL FRIEDMAN

Total campaign spending of all candidates in 1972 hit a record of $400 million. Senator John G. Tower, Republican of Texas, spent $2.5 million for his successful bid for re-election to the Senate. His opponent only spent $579,530. Just 60 seconds of prime time on CBS cost politicians up to $55,000. President Nixon raised $3.3 million in two high-priced dinners.

Photograph shows President and Mrs. Nixon giving smiles of victory at the Miami Republican Convention results. The President works tirelessly in an effort to achieve "a generation of peace." But those who are aware of prophetic Scripture realize we are living in the Last Days. Extremism will force upon the American people the narrow choice between anarchy and repression. The scene is already being set for Antichrist.

Turn to page 123 and you will see that beyond the exuberance of page 119 is a cancer that is slowing eating at the heart of America.

Henry Kissinger, President Nixon's foreign policy adviser, briefs the press in his famous October 26, 1972 debut with that now familiar phrase, "Peace is at hand."

While any President should be commended on his desire to seek peace... no President will be able to achieve such a goal in Vietnam nor in any other area of the world. Temporary stalemates may be called peace by some... but in reality, time will prove they are just a pause between an even greater conflict.

The Philadelphia Inquirer
Oldest Daily Newspaper in the United States—Founded 1771
Thursday, November 8, 1973
Vol. 289, No. 131
10 CENTS

Nixon Asks Power to Ration Fuel

Veto of War Powers Bill Overridden

By DAVID HESS

WASHINGTON—Congress Wednesday overrode President Nixon's veto of the war powers bill.

It was the first time in nine attempts that the Democratically controlled Congress has been able to overturn the Republican President's veto.

The vote dealt a staggering blow to an already weakened President, whose popular standing and credibility have dipped sharply in the turmoil surrounding the Watergate fi-

Congress Urged To Set 50 MPH Speed Limits

By ROBERT S. BOYD
Of Our Washington Bureau

WASHINGTON—President Nixon Wednesday proposed a wide-ranging energy conservation program that would give him standby authority to ration gasoline and fuel oil.

In a nationally televised speech, the President also asked the American people to drive slower, to turn down their thermostats to cope with what he called "the most acute shortages of energy since World War II."

In addition, the President asked Con

"All the News That's Fit to Print"

The New York Times

VOL. CXXII....No. 41,994   — NEW YORK, SUNDAY, JANUARY 14, 1973 —

Los Angeles Faces Strict Auto Curbs

By GLADWIN HILL
Special to The New York Times

LOS ANGELES, Jan. 13—The Environmental Protection Agency, under court orders, will prescribe drastic measures Monday for alleviating smog in Los Angeles by 1977.

The Federal formula is expected to include stringent gasoline rationing, possibly other restrictions on auto travel and the mandatory conversion of some commercial vehicles to nongasoline fuel.

The order is technically part of a federally required "implementation plan" by which the state of California, at least in theory, could comply with the Clean Air act of 1970 requiring national abatement of air pollution. It may presage similar Federal mandates covering other metropolitan areas that have excessive pollution from automotive or stationary sources.

"This is the crunch," a high-ranking official in Washington said this week. "This is the first dramatic confrontation between the Federal Government and the states on the 1970 act. People have to come to grips with the question of what price they want to pay for what benefits."

California

could lead to Congressional review of the air quality standards set under the 1970 act. At least of the 1977 deadline for state compliance.

The environmental agency's order will not become final until after public hearings are held in the affected area. Amendment of the order is discretionary with the Federal agency.

Hydrocarbons at Issue

Nominally the focal issue in California is how to reduce the amount of hydrocarbons in the Los Angeles basin below the Federal oxidant limit of .08 parts per million. Hydrocarbon is one of five basic types of air

among Congress, the environmental agency, the conservationists about whether the present national abatement program is too tough or not tough enough.

The law required states to submit to the Federal agency by last February comprehensive "implementation plans" for meeting Federal air quality standards by 1975. The law provided for two-year extensions of the target date, which have been granted to California and a number of other states.

The states were given until Feb. 15, 1973 to file detailed "strategies" for regulating transportation where necessary to reduce pollution.

PRICE RULE EASED FOR FOOD AND PR...

Exemptions and Add... to Pu...

By E... Special... WASH... though... mains a controls... Nixon... effort... in fac... for ..scribe P... are ... for Co...

KISSINGER

Inaugural will cost $4 million

Washington — Mr. Nixon's second inauguration and celebration either will be dull with sour overtones or promises to be surprisingly large and joyous — depending on from which of the President's two worlds you take soundings. Same reading for Vice President Spiro T. Agnew.

Expensive and big

It does seem to be a colossal inauguration. The President's reviewing stands on Pennsylvania Avenue, from where the President will review the two-mile long parade, cost $567,000 to construct. Among the 139 parade units will be 47 marching bands and 40 floats. Several concerts and two huge receptions are on the program. Frank Sinatra will serve as an emcee. Bob Hope, Sammy Davis Jr., James Brown, Zsa Zsa Gabor, the Pat Boone family, Hank Williams Jr., Van Cliburn and the Mike Curb Congregation are among the entertainers. Some 30,000 people are expected to attend a series of five inaugural balls, including one for youth.

The whole cost: a record $4 million, compared to $2.5 million spent in 1968.

...iladelphia Inquirer

...t Daily Newspaper in the United States—Founded 1771
SUNDAY MORNING, JANUARY 14, 1973   FINAL CITY EDE...

Rationing Looms In Oil Heat Crisis

Cutbacks Hit Homes, Industry

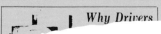

Why Drivers

Look at the photograph to the right. Your immediate reaction will give a clear indication of your own personal views.

If upon viewing the photo you say to yourself:

"Those pigs (policemen) are not allowing freedom of speech."

   chances are you are for a more permissive society

   and a downgrading of the police force.

   Carried to its furthest extension, this could lead to **anarchy**

   (political and social disorder due to absence of governmental control).

If, on the other hand, your initial reaction is:

"That hippie deserves to be hauled away between two night sticks."

   chances are you are for a society of more law and order

   and the institution of more restrictive measures.

   Carried to its furthest extension, this could pave the way for Antichrist

      and lead to a **dictatorship.**

   (a person exercising absolute power).

If you turn back to page 114 and reread Margaret Chase Smith's remarks you will recognize the fact that we are approaching an Un-United States.

A Christian should look at the photograph on page 123 with love and concern for both the policemen and the youth...and a desire to reach both with the Gospel of Jesus Christ. For the answer to peace lies not in permissiveness nor in repression but in a new life which begins at Calvary.

"Therefore if any man be in Christ, he is a new creature: old things are passed away; behold, all things are become new."   (2 Corinthians 5:17)

CLOUDY
Considerable cloudiness to-
day with a chance of showers.
High in the mid 70s.
Monday's Pollution Index—7
Average Spring Index—4 or 5
High ... 70
Low ... 60
Complete Weather on Page 21
TEN CENTS

The Philadelphia Inquirer

U. S. Could
Save Cities:
Humphrey
... Story, Page 8

THE OLDEST DAILY NEWSPAPER IN THE UNITED STATES—FOUNDED 1771

Vol. 284, No. 166   TUESDAY MORNING, JUNE 15, 1971   •   FINAL CITY EDITION

U. S. Demands N. Y. Times Halt War Study Publication

The New York Times said
Monday

Goldwater (R., Ariz.) said

ly equipped to go overseas

THE NEW YORK TIMES, THURSDAY, DECEMBER 10, 1971

Summary of Study on Changing, and Declining, Role of U.S. in World Economy

WASHINGTON, Dec. 29—
Following is the summary of
the study on the international

a nation and the world as
whole were too slow to realize that basic structural and
competitive changes were oc-

of interrelated problem areas.
They include:

**Trade With Developed
Countries**

Military Burden

Japan 0.8%

Military Expenditures* as
a Share of GNP, 1970

Study Proposes World Trade Changes

Continued From Page 1, Col. 1

loyalties and hopes of the weak-
er nations.

monetary systems "must" be
characterized by change but

THE NEW YORK TIMES, SUNDAY, NOVEMBER 19, 1972

218 Persons Involved in 159 U.S. Hijackings Since 1961, F.A.A. Says

By ROBERT LINDSEY

international diplomatic confer-

Roger Holder, 23 years old, and

Nixon's $500,000 Car: Like a Tank

From Our War Services

DETROIT — Built like a
tank, loaded with one-of-a-
kind options, and reportedly
built at a cost of $500,000,
President Nixon's new black
Lincoln Continental limousine
is ready for delivery by the
Ford Motor Co.

proof tires.
But if he chooses to stand to
wave, a bullet-proof plexiglas
bubble can be raised hydrauli-
cally from the top of the car.

THERE ARE HANDBARS
for Secret Service men. Running boards fold out from the

The climate of the United States has become so divisive that the President
must ride in a 1/2 Million Dollar car for protection. This two-tone photograph graphically shows how many people guard the President's
automobile.

Nader Says Congress Has Abdicated, Calls President a Kind of Monarch

By REM RIEDER

Bulletin Washington Bureau

Washington-- A study sponsored by consumer advocate Ralph Nader concludes that Congress is the "broken branch" of the Federal government.

The 286-page report, released last night, states that Congress has "abdicated" much of its power to the Ex-

from Capitol Hill to the grave and serious constitutional crisis." The White House under President Nixon is emerging as a "new kind of monarchy," he charged.

In response to a question, the nonpartisan Nader said he believed the Nixon Administration was "easily the most corrupt" in American history.

sympathetic to corporate interests, it is indentured to them," Nader said.

But he emphasized that he was not endorsing McGovern or ending his policy of avoiding partisan politics.

"We need the entire rotten government in this city changed," Nader said. "I'm not really interested in the presidential campaign."

Urges Reorganization

GOVERNMENT SECRETS REVEALED

In June, 1971 the world and particularly U.S. citizens were jolted when The New York Times released a secret Pentagon study of the Vietnam war.

This study revealed how the United States and particularly its leaders got this country embroiled in an Asian conflict. It was filled with intrigue, manipulating and clandestine actions.

It also brought to light once more the claim that "the government has a right to lie." Then when the report was printed by the TIMES, the Government immediately sought to clamp security on the entire document and to supress the truth.

What does this mean? This should reveal how large a gap of believability there is between press releases from government officials and the real truth. This also points to the fact that the fate of the entire nation rests on the whims and sometimes devious plans of a few in power.

No one knows what further documents, if they are ever released, will reveal...or what plans there are right now, for example...(a) to curb births by coercion, (b) to destroy the independence of evangelical churches, or (c) to enlarge the powers of the President.

We do know that all of this is shaping up to an all-powerful government which can control through manipulation of laws and information the life of each individual. This is but a short step from the powers that will be Antichrist's (Revelation 13). Watch out for those rosy fireside chats and those silver tongued orators. While they promise peace and prosperity...time will reveal more government control and more classified secret documents that will betray a nation's confidence.

Such actions only give more fuel to the liberal left and radicals...and a swing in either direction could spell persecution for the Christian.

Is it by chance or design that all cars owned by Arabs in Jerusalem must bear the prefix 666 on their license plate?

On the issuing of a Social Security number at age 6...

"Such a system would further enable the Government to amass information on citizens and store it in a central computer under a single identification number. To date, no one has suggested using tattoos."

TIME, March 13, 1972

The quotation on the left comes from a news article on a critical Senate Finance Committee vote. On March 3, 1972 the Senate Finance Committee voted to direct the U.S. Government to issue a Social Security card to every child entering the first grade after January 1, 1974. Its purpose is to make the Social Security number the universal form of identification for everyone in the U.S.

Such a system will enable the Government to begin to amass information on each individual at a very early age.

We have become acclimated to numbering systems. The first one to make a widespread use of a number was Adolf Hitler during World War 2. During that war he had the Jews tattooed with identification numbers on their forearms after they were placed in concentration camps.

Pick up the phone to make a telephone call. You dial an area code number. Mail a letter. You use a zip code number. Make a purchase in Sears or any large department store and your credit card with a number is punched into a special new computer that relays that number to a clearing house. Within a few split seconds the machine indicates whether your purchase is approved or denied.

Open a checking account...and your checks will bear a magnetic code number. Subscribe to a magazine...and you receive a computer number on a card which states, "Do not fold, spindle or mutilate."

In certain locations in Ohio, experiments have been conducted on making purchases in the local supermarket by a special magnetic card. After making purchases, the card is inserted into the computer. The clerk dials a number which connects his keyboard with the local bank. Within 15 seconds your purchases are either accepted...or, if your account is in arrears, you place the food back on the shelves!

Federal Government computers maintain millions of files covering every individual in the United States...and these are instantly available at the flick of a switch.

West Germany has already issued a 12-digit number to everyone in that country—this number will accompany its holder from cradle to grave.

I PREDICT by 1984

Most transactions will be made by a card identification system. Cash will become unpopular.

An invisible tattoo number system for identification will be introduced which becomes visible under special lights.

Says an official report: "The number has become vital to record-keeping in a number of federal agencies . . . Depending on where you live, you may find it on your local tax form, your bank account, your library card—even your dog's license-tag application."

Police from a mobile picture identification unit in Miami Beach photographing a demonstrator after mass arrests. Scene was the August, 1972 Republican convention.

YOUR NAME IS SURE TO BE IN ONE OF THESE COMPUTERS

The United States government knows you by a number. And federal agencies are turning to computers...which, at the touch of a button ...can produce instant information on millions of Americans. Here are some major examples:

SOCIAL SECURITY ADMINISTRATION
Your Social Security number will soon become a universal number.

INTERNAL REVENUE SERVICE
Computer tapes store details from tax returns of over 75 million citizens. These tapes are made available to the 50 States.

U.S. SECRET SERVICE
About 50,000 persons are on computer who might tend to harm or embarrass the President or other high Government officials.

F.B.I.
Fingerprint files of over 86 million people now on computer.

DEPARTMENT OF AGRICULTURE
Keeps data on over 850,000 people.

DEPARTMENT OF TRANSPORTATION
Almost 2.7 million citizens who have been denied driver's licenses are on computer.

PENTAGON
Maintains files on some 7 million military personnel and civilians who have been subjected to "security, loyalty, criminal and other type investigations."

VETERANS ADMINISTRATION
Keeps files on 13.5 million veterans and dependents.

DEPARTMENT OF LABOR
Has on computer files on 2 million persons in federally financed work...all coded by their social security number.

DEPARTMENT OF JUSTICE
Computer bank has names of more than 14,000 individuals who have been involved in riots and civil disorders since mid-1968.

DEPARTMENT of HOUSING and URBAN DEVELOPMENT
Maintains records on 4.5 million who have bought F.H.A. homes.

With this federal computer network, there is virtually no limit to the volume of information that can be made available at a moment's notice on just about every American.

DESCRIPTION OF CHARGES	TOTAL CHARGES	BLUE CROSS OR OTHER INSURANCE COVERAGE	PATIENT'S CHARGES
47 DAYS AT 113.00	5,311.00	4,620.10	690.90
63 DAYS AT 121.00	7,623.00	5,209.90	2,413.10
ROOM AND BOARD	12,934.00	9,830.00	3,104.00
LABORATORY	2,177.40	2,062.90	114.50
X-RAY	852.00	852.00	
PHARMACY	800.80	653.80	147.00
MEDICAL & SURGICAL SUPPLY	413.55	405.55	8.00
INHALATION THERAPY	20.00	10.00	10.00
CARDIOGRAM	35.00	35.00	
X-RAY THERAPY	1,085.00		1,085.00
PHONE	20.78		20.78
TOTAL CHARGES	18,338.53	14,223.50	4,115.03

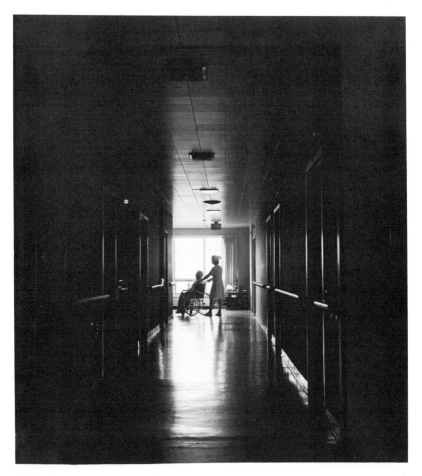

YOU NO LONGER CAN AFFORD THE Luxury of GETTING SICK!

Look at a typical bill from a New York hospital...to the left.

For 110 days in the hospital (and the patient died) the total charges were $18,338.53.

Over $18 thousand for a little over 3 months in a hospital! One could have purchased a nice home for that amount of money or a Rolls Royce plus a new Cadillac. Or you could have lived 3 1/2 years drawing $100 a week on retirement! Or you could have lived in a plush hotel for **almost 1 year at $50 a day** in a luxury suite with room service and meals!

Just 10 years ago the average hospital stay cost the patient $265. Today the average hospital stay costs the patient $785!

Hospital rates have risen five-fold. Today they are hovering at about $100 a day! In 10 years I PREDICT hospital rates will be $1000 a day!

Already in a Boston hospital rates for one day are as high as $425.75! Doctors are the most highly paid professionals in the country. They earn a median income of $40,000 a year...after expenses and before taxes. Only 1% of Americans earn as much as this. But doctors are now also faced with medical malpractice suits. And some pay as high as a $5000 premium annually for malpractice insurance.

Coupled with the rise in hospital costs the United States is now in the grip of at least 2 vast epidemics — venereal disease and heart disease. Heart disease is the nation's No. 1 cause of death, taking 700,000 lives and costing more than $30 Billion a year!

* * *

Americans have become so infused with drugs (both legal prescription and illegal narcotics) that at least 1.5 million hospital admissions a year are caused by bad reactions to medicinal drugs. American drug companies produce 8 billion pills a YEAR, or 40 for every man, woman and child in the United States.

What does this mean? The growing drug epidemic is alarming government officials. We are already witnessing a nation that in the last 3 years has experienced one violence after another...angry rebellions. The Achilles heel of our nation has been wounded. This will bring about more government control; more power in the hands of one man, the President. In the Tribulation Period, those without the Mark will be refused such things as hospital care (Revelation 13:16-18). Can you imagine the horror of that day?

Sydney J. Harris

Wanted--a False Messiah

Reprinted by request.

People keep saying "We need a leader" or "We need better leadership," but that is not what they really mean. What most of them are looking for is not a leader, but a Messiah.

They want someone who will give them the Word. And the Word would be one that is agreeable to them, that appeals to their preferences and prejudices, so they can follow it wholeheartedly.

the common good and for the good of their own souls. He is never followed by very many, usually killed by the majority, and venerated only when he is safely dead and need not be taken seriously.

What we are looking for, I am afraid, is neither a true leader nor a true Messiah, but a false Messiah — a man who will give us over-simplified answers, who will justify our ways, who will castigate our enemies, who will vindicate our selfishness as a way of life, and make us comfortable within our

'Chromosome Passports'
For All Forecast by Experts

JERUSALEM, Sept. 16 (Agence France-Presse)—Scientist here forecast this week that before long every person would carry a "chromosome passport" issued at birth by a computerized machine.

Professionally called a karyotype, the passport would contain the genetic analysis of the individual and would be carried like blood-group tags by soldiers and many civilians, the scientists said. Couples contemplating marriage will be expected to exchange karyotypes as well as general health certificates.

This was forecast at the fourth international chromosome conference in Jerusalem, attended by 150 participants from 22 countries.

GREATER GOVERNMENT CONTROL FORESEEN

Some believe that the best way to solve a problem is for the government (fellow human beings from Washington) to take over and control the situation. This works out fine as long as you are in agreement with the controls applied to the particular situation.

But when the control restricts your freedom, then it becomes another story.

If you read your newspapers carefully with the idea of trying to project the news into future events...you will find that when the U.S. government is able to prohibit a document from being published...it may also in the future be able to prohibit Christians from printing the Gospel. This may seem difficult for you to believe...but we already are seeing a growing resentment against Christians by many who are blaming them for the ecology crisis.

A June, 1971 REDBOOK article quoted Lynn White, Jr., a historian at the University of California, as saying that "Christianity made it possible to exploit nature in a mood of indifference."

Further on it is stated that "the advent of Christianity...led us to the present crisis."

Continued thinking of this nature will prove dangerous to Christians. Suppose, as an example, someone is elected into the Presidency or high governmental office who really believes that the pollution crisis of the earth today is due to the "strange beliefs of the Christians."

If a government can supress news, control and commit over half a million men to a war in Asia, it is not unreasonable to believe that this same government can control and persecute Christians. This is exactly what will occur in the tribulation period! (Matthew 24:15-22)

2 Frenchmen Are Executed By Guillotine

Paris — (AP) — Two convicts who cut the throats of two hostages in an attempted prison break were guillotined at dawn today in Sante Prison after President Georges Pompidou for the first time refused to commute death sentences.

Claule Buffet, 39, and Roger Bontempts, 45, were the first persons to be executed in France since March 1960. Pompidou, who opposes the death penalty, took office in June 1969.

The two men were accused of killing a guard and a prison nurse in Clairvaux Prison on Sept. 21, 1971.

Presumably a rash of disturbances in French prisons recently was a factor in Pompidou's refusal of clemency.

The above news article appeared November 28, 1972. Could this be a foreshadowing of the method of execution to be used in the Tribulation Period on those who refuse to accept the Mark?

...and I saw the souls to them that were beheaded for the witness of Jesus, and for the word of God, and which had not worshipped the beast, neither his image, neither had received his mark upon their foreheads, or in their hands, and they lived and reigned with Christ a thousand years" (Revelation 20:4).

134

MODERN DAY BABYLON?

Where will the forces of antichrist emerge...from London? from the rebuilt Babylon in Iraq? from Rome or from New York City?

Is the photograph on the next page a preview of things to come? This office building in the heart of Manhattan was photographed by the author at dusk.

New York City...the city that built a revolutionary dinosaur, the World Trade Center, equipped with 6500 remote sensors that feed information on temperature, humidity, pressure, water flow and power needs to a master computer. Its two tall buildings rise 100 feet higher than the Empire State building. It uses as much electrical power each day as the entire city of Stamford, Connecticut. This $700 million complex houses 50,000 employees and has 80,000 visitors daily!

New York City...where offtrack betting was introduced and where annually some 18 million visitors spend almost $2 billion.

New York City...where people paid $20 to scalpers for $4 tickets to see "The Godfather," a motion picture glorifying crime which initially grossed $1 million a day!

New York City...where power failures send 40 million gallons of raw sewage into Jamaica Bay...while millions of dollars of pornagraphic sewage flows down 42nd Street.

Will New York City become the modern day Babylon? Time will tell.

As of January, 1973
here are the COMMON MARKET nations:

Great Britain	France	Italy
Ireland	Luxembourg	Belgium
Denmark	West Germany	Netherlands

"When we conquer on a world scale, I think we shall use gold for the purpose of building public lavatories in the streets of large cities."

Lenin

In December, 1971 finance chiefs of the 10 richest non-Communist nations announced an agreement on a new system of money exchange. This exchange featured the devaluation of the U.S. dollar by 8.57%. For the first time in current history, America became a follower and no longer a leader. The United States was forced to bow to the demands of primarily the European Common Market nations. In fact, U.S. officials are in favor of doing away with gold as a monetary standard. Right now so-called "paper gold" is being issued by the International Monetary Fund (IMF) as an increasingly popular substitute.

Today there are 9 nations in the Common Market. In July, 1972 the Common Market and the European Free Trade Association formerly merged in a treaty-signing ceremony that produced a free trade zone for 300 million people.

These 9 Common Market nations are stronger than the U.S. from a standpoint of (1) population, (2) Gross National Product, (3) exports, (4) imports, (5) the production of iron and steel, (6) automobiles, and (7) available work force.

They are not stronger militarily. Since the Common Market nations hold the purse strings...having forced the U.S. to lower its currency through *devaluation*...the United States must depend more and more on these nations *for its* economic health. Such a dilemma may yet force the United States into joining the Common Market nations into what may be called a United States of Europe—or perhaps their official name might become, UNITED STATES EUROPE, or:

AMERICA-EUROPE
U   N   I   T   E   D

It is forseeable that such an American-European conglomerate would be headed by one powerful figure known in Scriptures as ANTI-CHRIST. There are presently 9 nations in the Common Market. This is not necessarily the final federation of the U.S. of Europe. However the grouping of European nations into a 9 unit Common Market indicates that these nations are no longer thinking individually but are at last cooperating as a singular force. Out of this can evolve the final United States of Europe comprised of 10 nations—the Revived Roman Empire of Biblical Prophecy (Daniel 7:23-24)!

Common Market nations are now seeking a single monetary system to be used by every member nation. And while the U.S. is losing its gold, other nations, including Russia, are piling it up—driving us into further desperation nearer to waiting (?) European arms.

I PREDICT by 1991 — The United States will join the free European nations into what will become known as UNITED STATES EUROPE.

The New York Times

Weather: Possible light snow today;
cloudy tonight. Warmer tomorrow.
Temp. range: today 17-31; Saturday
13-30. Full U.S. report on Page 71.

SECTION ONE

VOL. CXXI . . No. 41,602   NEW YORK, SUNDAY, DECEMBER 19, 1971   50 CENTS

10-NATION MONETARY AGREEMENT REACHED;
DOLLAR IS DEVALUED 8.57%; SURCHARGE OFF

Pakistan Calls Bhutto to Form Regime With New Charter

YAHYA DENOUNCED	REDISTRICTING BILL HELPFUL TO G.O.P.	NIXON HAILS PACT
Approval by President of Cong...	PASSED IN ALBANY	He Makes a Surprise Appearance—Gold Goes to $38

President Nixon returns from Azores after dollar devaluation announcement. With him are Secretary of State Rogers, former Secretary of the
Treasury John Connally and Henry Kissinger.

ARE U.S. AND EUROPE
NEARING A SHOWDOWN?

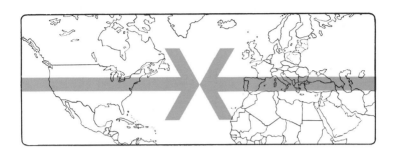

IS THIS THE BEGINNING OF THE END FOR THE UNITED STATES?

Recently we have seen the number 10 crop up more frequently than ever before in world movements. This headline from the December 19, 1971 issue of THE NEW YORK TIMES is another example of this.

President Nixon's report to the nation on the devaluation of the United States dollar was filled with glowing terms. One might think in reading the text of the speech that this was the greatest achievement in current history...

But I PREDICT, the devaluation of the U.S. dollar is the beginning of America's decline as a major world force!

I PREDICT that no longer will America be leading the way economically nor militarily.

I PREDICT that a 10 nation federation of European States (the Common Market) will yet someday lead the world economically and politically!

The President, in his official text said:

"Now we have a new world, fortunately a much better world economically, where instead of just one strong economic nation, the nations of Europe, Japan and Asia, Canada and North America, all these nations are strong economically...."

He began his text by saying: "...it is my very great privilege to announce on behalf of the finance ministers and the other representatives of the 10 countries involved, the conclusion of the most significant monetary agreement in the history of the world."

I agree...it is the most significant monetary agreement...an agreement that has found most Americans asleep...hailing it as a triumph...when in reality it is a TRAGEDY! A tragedy that is the beginning of the end for the United States! For the U.S. with its once great ideals is now beginning to relinquish its role as world leader and defender of world freedom. With the abdication of this leadership role the ideals are also being abandoned.

Europe's Dollar 'Tea Party'

American tourists in London queue outside American Express office, August 1971, to convert their traveler's checks into sterling during dollar devaluation crisis.

THE NEW YORK TIMES, SATURDAY, MAY 22, 1971

New Europe Being Born, and Nothing Will Be the Same Again

By ANTHONY LEWIS

St. Louis Globe-Democrat

120 Years of Public Service / Founded July 1, 1852

Friday, October 20, 1972   42 Pages

U.S. faces business war with Europe

By ARTHUR L. GAVSHON
Associated Press Writer

9 Common Market nations pledge in summit to unify money, trade and foreign policies

LONDON SEEKS COMMON MARKET LEADERSHIP

Three years ago people were saying that England didn't stand the ghost of a chance to enter the Common Market.

Now London is vying for leadership in the cooperative group of European nations. And no city in Europe can quite match the square mile of the "City" of London...the financial district.

They have erected a new 26-story building which they hope will serve for this purpose. London has become the center not only for European currency exchange but now also for U.S. currency. London has the world's largest shipping and air chartering market. It has the most important stock market in Europe.

Where will Antichrist make his headquarters? We do not know. The United States? Babylon? Jerusalem? London? Rome? Certain recent events would seem to indicate that London stands as good a chance as any of once again becoming the focal point of world finance.

Common Market Headquarters in Brussels, Belgium.

143

Japan's youth, protesting U.S. involvement in Asia, lay a Tokyo street under barricade with an overturned car. The police in aluminum gladiator shields await the next onslaught.

"China alone of all nations of the world could well afford to suffer two or three hundred million casualties, and so has least reason to fear nuclear retaliation."

Chairman Mao

"Mr. Chamberlain thinks that if he feeds the crocodile often enough, this beast will eventually be satisfied; in reality the crocodile's appetite will become so voracious from these frequent feedings that it will never be sated short of devouring Mr. Chamberlain and the whole of Europe."

Winston Churchill upon Neville Chamberlain's return to London with umbrella in hand and smile on his face after signing the Munich Pact in his "Journey for Peace."

Two sleeping giants are awakening! China and Japan. And soon their thundering footsteps may shake the entire earth in bloody wars!

In February, 1972, President Nixon went to Red China in what he termed a "Journey for Peace." Time will prove otherwise.

In the last 50 years Chinese Communism has been responsible for the murder of at least 35 million lives...possibly as many as 50 million! Many of these—perhaps millions—were our Christian brethren who were martyred for Christ. Only God knows how many—as the communists annihilated the entire professing Church in China in one generation.

In spite of this Red China gained prestige and recognition when in October, 1971 she was officially admitted into the UN...and Taiwan was unceremoniously ousted.

Now Red China is enlarging its ring of influence...by increasing her foreign aid to countries that eventually will prove a stepping stone to the Middle East...and OIL. Actually Red China's financial aid in 1970 alone to developing nations reached $709 million - surpassing even the Soviet Union's much smaller $204 million!

Red China's tentacles reach into many African countries including Zambia and Tanzania. 7000 Red Chinese alone were dispatched to Tanzania to build a railroad from Dar Es Salaam to the rich Zambian copper belt.

On April 2, 1972, 100,000 people in Peking greeted the Prime Minister of Malta. Malta is the smallest nation in the world. Yet Red China extended a loan with no strings attached.

China may one day use Malta as her stepping off place for an invasion of Israel. Red China already has missiles that can reach Moscow and the Middle East. And even Israel has shown a desire for establishing closer relations with this power of the East.

Red China's biggest fear is Japan. The "smart bombs" used by the United States in 1972 on North Vietnam...bombs that always hit their target...contained Sony TV units. It's this type of technology that makes Japan a threatening world force.

As China fears Japan, so also, Japan fears China. This is why the recent U.S. recognition of Red China has forced Japan into an alliance with China in order to exist. This is so because a United States at peace with Red China could not be depended upon to help Japan in any Japanese-Chinese confrontation. Japan, once our ally, will soon again become our enemy.

I PREDICT by 1975
Red China will take over Taiwan.
A war will break out in Korea.
China will have a 6000 mile missile range capability.

The Evening Bulletin

INDEPENDENT—LOCALLY OWNED

WITH SUNDAY MORNING EDITION

PHILADELPHIA, PA. 19101, TUESDAY, OCTOBER 26, 1971 — DAILY HOME DELIVERY 50 CENTS PER WEEK — TEN CENTS

UN Ousts Taiwan and Admits Red China

Longshoremen — Senators Push — **Major Defeat**

Nixon Leaves for Peking
On 'Journey for Peace'

President

Vol. 266, No. 59 — MONDAY MORNING, FEBRUARY 28, 1972 — FINAL CITY EDITION

One Observation: They Got Taiwan; We Got Eggroll

By ROBERT S. BOYD

Our Man in China

Robert S. Boyd, Chief of our Washington Bureau

SHANGHAI—In the short run President Nixon gave more than he got in his "week that changed the world" in the Peoples Republic of China.

Eventual Taiwan Pullout Pledged

President
Recognizes
One China

By STANLEY KARNOW

The Evening News

No. 17,078—36 PAGES — HARRISBURG, PENNA., MONDAY, FEBRUARY 28, 1972 — PRICE TEN CENTS

Future of Chiang's regime in doubt

'The week that changed the world...'

The scoreboard

How Nixon and Chou stand on key points of five-day summit

SHANGHAI (AP)—Here are the viewpoints of the United States and the Peoples Republic of China as expressed in a communique summing up five days of talks between President Nixon and Premier Chou En-lai last week in Peking.

Chinese remain firm in support of North Vietnam

By PETER LISAGOR
Special To The Evening News
And Chicago Daily News

RED CHINA and The UNITED STATES
"The Spider and the Fly"

In the opinion of this writer, the United States has made a grievous error in courting RED CHINA.

You cannot do business with the Devil and win! You can do a great deal of business with him. You can become further and further involved. Your tricky diplomatic maneuvers may seemingly even give you the edge. Soon, however, you become so enmeshed like a fly in a web that there is no escape.

Atheistic Red China, like Russia, has one goal...world conquest. Red China has already firmly established strongholds in most of the nations of AFRICA. Her "agricultural assistance" teams have won many African nations to her side. In the meantime, Russia has won many friends among the Arab nations.

NOW DO YOU GET THE PICTURE...prophetically? Can you see what this is all leading up to—for the Tribulation Period?

Russia and her allies...with Arab nations as friends...will converge on Israel in one conflict (Ezekiel 38:1-39:16).

Red China with possibly Japan will move up on Israel from the East— possibly planning to utilize African bases (Revelation 16:12).

And the United States? Perhaps it will be part of the 10 Nation European Federation...dominated by Antichrist (Revelation 17:12)? Time will tell.

One question!

WHO STANDS TO LOSE MOST IN A NUCLEAR WAR?

China? NO
Russia? NO

The UNITED STATES would suffer the greatest casualties!

Why? Because the United States has the **greatest concentration** of people living in urban areas.

Look at this:

73% of the **total population** in the United States lives in city (urban) areas!

56% of the total population of Russia live in urban areas.

But only 15% of the total population of Red China lives in urban areas.

RED CHINA already has some 150 nuclear bombs and missile warheads. It is estimated that within 2 years Red China will have intercontinental-range missiles.

Now can you see from a political standpoint why the United States has changed its diplomatic attitude towards Red China?

PEKING
REVIEW

7-8

February 25, 1972

Chairman Mao Meets President Nixon

The Principle of Acupunctural
Anaesthesia

Diplomatic Relations Established Between
China and Mexico and Between
China and Argentina

PEKING
REVIEW

14

April 7, 1972

**Prime Minister Mintoff of Malta
Welcomed in China**

Statement of the Chinese Ministry
Of Foreign Affairs

March 31, 1972

Mass Physical Training

Chou Declares U.S. Is Losing Pre-eminent Position in World

a. 1973 The Globe and Mail, Toronto

PEKING, Aug. 28—Premier Chou En-lai declared last night that the United States is on the verge of losing the pre-eminent position it has enjoyed in world affairs since the end of World War II.

The Premier said at a banquet here that "the whole world is in the midst of a great upheaval, and the situation is excellent." He added: "The United States imperialst position of hegemony established after World War II has been shaken to its very foundation, and the imperialist colonial position is collapsing."

It was the second time in recent weeks that a Chinese leader has spoken of "a great upheaval" in world affairs. The phrase was also used by Huang Yung-shen, the army chief of staff, when he welcomed a visiting North Korean military delegation to Peking on Aug. 18.

from Indochina, together with growing isolationist sentiment among the American voters, has create a fluid situation in which they can score significant diplomatic gains.

Mr. Chou's remarks came at a banquet in honor of Ieng Sary, a special envoy of Prince Norodom Sihanouk's Cambodian government in exile Mr. Sary is on a visit to Peking from the guerrilla-controlled area of Cambodia.

The 73-year-old Premier also attacked the Soviet union though not by name and with sufficient indirection that Soviet diplomats who were present did not feel obliged to walkout, as they have on similar occasions in the past.

"The power politics practiced by the superpowers have met with universal opposition from medium and small countries" Mr. Chou said.

"Voices for defending state...... national observers her...

Peking Offers $42M Loan To Mediterranean Island

VALETTA, Malta (UPI) — Prime Minister Dom Mintoff said last night that China has offered Malta a $42.6 million loan package that gives Peking its first toehold in the Mediterranean.

Mintoff, who visited China earlier this month, told Parliament the no-interest, no-conditions loan will start within five days and run for six years.

Distinguished Maltese Guests Warmly Welcomed

ONE hundred thousand people in Peking on April 2 gave Prime Minister Dominic Mintoff and the Maltese Government Delegation he led a warm welcome. They expressed firm support for the Maltese Government and people in their just struggle welcome to the Maltese Government Delegation!" "Firm support to the Maltese Government and people in their just struggle to safeguard their state sovereignty and national independence!" "Long live the friendship between the peoples of China and Malta!" and "Long

---

(I receive PEKING REVIEW every week)

It revealed that when the President of the United States (the **most powerful** country in the world) came to CHINA ONLY A HANDFUL Welcomed Him!

BUT, when Prime Minister Mintoff, (representing MALTA, the **smallest** country in the world), came to CHINA 100,000 CHINESE Greeted Him!

WHY

would RED CHINA show more interest in the smallest country in the world, MALTA...than in the United States? Can you find MALTA on your map? Why not search for it right now!

PEKING gave MALTA over $42 MILLION DOLLARS at **no** interest and with **no** conditions!

Reason: MALTA is the gateway to the Mediterranean and the Middle East! Can you see how the alignment of nations for ARMAGEDDON is already heading!

DID THIS TOAST

President Nixon and Chou En-lai toast each other during the President's visit to Peking, February 1972. Will history show that this meeting opened a Pandora's box which gave birth to the Asiatic Confederacy?

CEMENT THIS ALLIANCE?

Chou En-Lai and Prime Minister Kakuei Tanaka of Japan toast each other. In late September, 1972, Tanaka, known as "the computerized bulldozer," apologized to the Chinese people, established diplomatic relations with Red China and absolved Japan's treaty with Taiwan.

Grandfatherly Chairman Mao, dedicated to the conquest of his free and peaceful neighbors, was responsible for the murder of over 34 million persons in Red China who disagreed with him.

WORLD PATTERN of DOMINATION forms
for the coming Tribulation Period

The admission of Red China into the UN was a major defeat for the United States.

And President Nixon's trip to China may on the surface be a political victory, but it may culminate in a national disaster.

Roosevelt compromised with Russia and we had a disastrous YALTA Conference.

Kennedy compromised with Russia and we had a Berlin Wall and Cuban crisis.

Recognizing China and opening the door gives that country additional political power and an air of respectability which it (a mass murderer of Christians) does not deserve.

Politically American friendship with China pits Russia against China in a bid for attention from the West. But this will backfire as the two finally get together and converge both against the nation of Israel and against the Western powers. For a while...until God intervenes...they will have the last laugh.

Communist China's first step upon entering the UN was to make their **very first speech one of condemnation of the United States!** And they then listed a set of demands for which they would fight.

I PREDICT
RED CHINA will step up her demands that Taiwan (Free China) become a part of Red China.

RED CHINA will step up her demands that U.S. forces be withdrawn from Asia.

RED CHINA will step up her demands that U.S. release trade restrictions immediately.

I PREDICT
facts later on will prove that the President's visit to Red China was not the triumph initially claimed...but a tragedy that will further set America back as a leader. It will contribute measurably to making the U.S. a follower rather than a pace-setter in world leadership.

I PREDICT
future events will prove the China meeting was the beginning of our acquiescing to the demands of China...but the enormity of this tragedy will not be realized until a year or two after the Presidential election.

RED CHINA will one day march on Israel to destroy her (Revelation 16:12).

ASIA'S ADVANCE IN THE MIDDLE EAST via AFRICA

Africa will be much in the news. And though it may not appear so... Africa will, in my opinion, have a major role in the Tribulation Period.

In 1972 envoy Yang Shoucheng of Communist China made a secret 4-Day visit to Ethiopia and met with Emperor Haile Selassie and leaders of his government. Emperor Selassie in the past has been known for his friendship to the United States and for his sympathy to the Christian cause. No one knows exactly what happened at this 4-Day meeting. The results of the meeting are known, however. The Ethiopian Government has announced it has recognized the Communist Chinese regime as the **sole** legal government of **all** the Chinese people.

Look at your map. Ethiopia is in a strategic position...near the Red Sea which flows north through the Suez Canal. Its population is over 25 million people and its land area covers almost 480,000 square miles. Ethiopia has valuable mineral reserves, including gold and platinum.

LET'S SET THE SCENE....

At the close of the Tribulation Period Israel will find herself being invaded by 200 million warriors. An army will come from the east (Asia) perhaps to contest the right of the Federation States of Europe to have world-wide dominion. There has always been friction between China and the Western nations. And it is quite possible that Japan may join China in a move to dump Antichrist and to take control over the world. The scene of this final battle will be Armegeddon! (Revelation 16:12-16)

From a human standpoint, you might say...why would China...way over on the other side of the world try to transport millions of men way over to Israel? That's a good question. And that's why I suggest that AFRICA may be the key to this answer!

RIGHT NOW....China is laying the groundwork in Africa for a possible sweep up through the African states approaching Israel from the south ...for the Endtime conflict.

Let me show you what is happening right now in Africa under the behind-the-scenes maneuvering of the Red Chinese.

Quietly, under the guise of technical assistance...Red China has been sending trained men to many of the countries of Africa to show them how to grow better crops, how to industrialize their nation.

China is investing millions in aid to African nations and winning many of them over to her side. There are at least 15 nations in Africa that have diplomatic ties with Red China.

And while Pakistan may not be considered part of Africa...when this country was hit by a tidal wave in 1971...Red China was the first country, through its Red Cross, to send money...over ONE MILLION DOLLARS!

As a result, many of the votes to recognize Red China in the United Nations have come from African countries.

No one knows how many Red Chinese there are in Africa. All we do know is that there are many thousands. Passing themselves off as agricultural and industrial technicians...there is no doubt that many of them are secret agents preparing the way for Communist domination of these countries. Yes, the anti-colonial communists are vying even with one another—Russia vs. China—to gain spheres of influence in Africa!

If you look on a map of Africa...you will see there is a DIRECT LINE of Red China-sympathetic nations which points right to Israel. Starting from the extreme south of Africa and moving in a line northward... here are the countries which have diplomatic ties with Red China:

Zambia, Tanzania, Kenya, Uganda, Ethiopia, Sudan, United Arab Republic...and north of Israel you have Syria and Iraq. Now there are other countries in this African segment that recognize Red China and have Chinese working in their country...but the above countries are the ones that put a direct pincer approach on Israel and would make it possible for Red Chinese forces to have a clear approach in a southern invasion attempt.

COUPLE THIS WITH THE FACT that Japan is the fastest-growing major industrial power in the world. In the 1960's Japan surpassed Italy, France and Germany as well as England. If her total industrial output continues at the pace it is now going it will surpass RUSSIA in 1979 and surpass the United States before 1990! Now, if Japan unites its forces with China...and there is reason to believe that this is possible... this Asian bloc will be powerful beyond belief.

Can you see why it may be necessary for the United States to merge with 9 other European nations in order to maintain a power balance?

Secretary of State William P. Rogers displays the historic document he signed at the State Department restoring Okinawa to Japanese sovereignity. Standing behind Rogers, from left, are Secretary of Army Resor, Undersecretary of State, Johnson and Secretary of Defense, Melvin R. Laird. Signing took place June 17, 1972.

China Quietly Renewing An Active Role in Africa

By WILLIAM BORDERS
Special to The New York Times

LAGOS, Nigeria, April 8—A Chinese Communist diplomat, Chang Li, came to this sultry capital the other day to open an embassy, establishing diplomatic relations with Nigeria and marking what many regard as a turning point in the Peking Government's relations with Africa.

"The Chinese had been quiet and stagnant all over the continent since the middle sixties," explained a Western diplomat who counts China-watching

¶The inauguration of a $400,-million Chinese railway project in Tanzania and Zambia, illustrating renewed aid potential.

Peking is winning new friends among the Africans, from the rice paddies of Mauritania, where Chinese agronomists are improving the yield, to the whitewashed Lenin Hospital overlooking the Indian Ocean in Zanzibar, 4,000 miles away, where Chinese doctors are fighting disabling tropical diseases.

China Is Looking to Japan For Industrial Know-How

Relays of Specialists Explore Tokyo's Technology to Implement Peking's Fourth 5-Year Economic Plan

By JUNNOSUKE OFUSA
Special to The New York Times

TOKYO, Nov. 12 — With Japan's diplomatic recognition of China, the Chinese have begun an intensive effort to acquire Japanese industrial technology.

It has become apparent that, aside from political reasons, a major Chinese objective is her principal source of imports.

Under the fourth five-year plan, which ends in 1975, China plans to modernize her steel, machinery, automobile and shipbuilding industries, in addition to developing air, overland and maritime transportation.

To promote the program, China would not only import shipping, steel and other industrial products from Japan but also expand and modernize her industries with Japanese technology.

Peking has already requested two major Japanese steel manufacturers to submit written estimates for building a sophisticated continuous rolling mill

U.S. Officials Say China Widens African Aid to Extend Influence

By TAD SZULC
Special to The New York Times

WASHINGTON, Sept. 3—China has negotiated or renewed aid and trade agreements with 24 African countries in the last two years, closely following the resumption of active diplomacy after the isolation of the Cultural Revolution in the late nineteen-sixties.

According to information compiled by United States specialists, Peking is concentrating on expanding economic relations with Algeria, Egypt, the Sudan, Ethiopia, Tanzania and Zambia, demonstrating con-

Egypt, which has mounting problems with Moscow, is a case in point. Chinese-Egyptian trade, which had totaled $12.5-million a year, is to be increased to $85-million in an agreement signed last March.

In the Sudan, China supplied Khartoum with $80-million in loans, after an attempted takeover of the Government, reportedly backed by Moscow, failed. A trade agreement signed in May provided for $70-million in annual trade exchanges.

Ethiopia received $87.5-million in loans from China last October and a Peking commitment to purchase a large

Soap traditionally imported by Tanzania from Kenya was re-

New Zealand Pulling Out Of SEATO, Leader Says

Wellington, New Zealand—(AP) — Prime Minister-elect Norman Eric Kirk says he will take New Zealand out of the Southeast Asia Treaty Organization.

"There will be a lot of changes," Kirk, 49, said in an

北京　Peking and Jerusalem　耶路撒冷

'Israel scientist aided China, for a year'

HAIFA. — A "senior" Israeli scientist went to Communist China in 1963 to help the Chinese solve "various scientific problems," former Premier David Ben-Gurion said here last night.

He said the Chinese made "tremendous strides" in the development of military technology during the time the Israeli scientist was there, which he said was more than one year. The Israeli was a faculty member of the Hebrew University, Mr. Ben-Gurion said, and was invited to visit China by that country's government.

B-G was speaking at a meeting of Hagana veterans in Haifa.

Israel, China Plan Telephone Link

JERUSALEM (UPI). — A long-distance telephone link between Israel and Communist China will be inaugurated July 1, an Israeli Communications Ministry spokesman said Tuesday.

The spokesman said the move was merely an "expansion of service to subscribers" and had no political significance.

Israel and Communist China do not maintain diplomatic relations.

A member of Mao Tsetung's Thought propaganda team stationed at a primary school...takes his students on a tour. Note both pupils and teacher carry Chairman Mao's Red Book!

Tanaka Defends Doubling Of Military Budget by '76

By RICHARD HALLORAN
Special to The New York Times

TOKYO, Oct. 11 — Premier Kakuei Tanaka of Japan gave more evidence today that he intends to lead Japan toward an independent and vigorous defense and foreign policy.

Mr. Tanaka, who set the outlines of that policy in his meetings with President Nixon and Premier Chou En-lai of China last month, defended his Government's plan to double military spending over the next five years.

The P—

for the same reason, had been urging the Japanese Government to buy in America, arguing that American-made planes are cheaper than those that would be produced in Japan because the investment in production facilities has already been made.

The Defense Agency, backed by many Japanese industrialists, however, contended that Japan should build her own defense production facilities ac-

TANAKA IS SEEKING WORLDWIDE TRUST

Japanese Premier Foresees Role as a Donor of Aid— Domestic Aims Set Too

By RICHARD HALLORAN
Special to The New York Times

TOKYO, Oct. 28—Premier Kakuei Tanaka of Japan, in his first comprehensive address since taking office in July, said today, "I intend to exert all efforts to build a country that will be trusted more than ever by the nations of the world and which will become the joy of each person who was born

Japan's Military Forces Winning Public Approval

TOKYO, Nov. 14 (Reuters)—Public opinion here once more considers it respectable to wear a Japanese military uniform.

Alongside this growing public acceptance, a major build-up in Japan's self-defense forces, as they are called, appears likely in the current decade.

But the disastrous course of national politics under military influence in World War II has

by as much as 90 per cent of its planned complement.

But much of the increased allocation will pay for modern weapons.

The defense white paper pledges that Japan never will acquire any weapons of aggression, while the present Constitution also limits military forces to defense of the homeland. Japanese troops could not even take part in an international

China's greatest fear is the military growth of Japan. This photo shows missiles of Japan's Self-Defense Force paraded through Tokyo.

Japan Tightens Her Economic Grip
On Nations of East and South Asia

By JAMES P. STERBA

Special to The New York Times

SINGAPORE, Aug. 21—With a speed and intensity that has sent chills through her neighbors, Japan has emerged as the pre-eminent economic force over East and Southeast Asia —a force with overwhelming power and little competition.

diversifying her markets and import sources to depend on them less and less.

At the beginning of an era in world relations expected by many world leaders to be dominated by economic rather than political or military might, Japan appears to have no peers among the major powers as

It is almost impossible in Hong Kong and Singapore to look out a window without seeing a great neon plug for Sanyo, Seiko, National, Sony, Teijin, Datsun, or Mitsubishi.

In Bangkok, a Thai businessman wakes up by a Japanese alarm clock, looks out a window made of Japanese,

U.S.-Japanese Deal Is Set on Soviet Gas

By THEODORE SHABAD

Special to The New York Times

MOSCOW, Oct. 29—An ambitious United States-Japanese deal for the development of Siberian natural resources appeared to be shaping up here last week as executives from the two countries met separately with Soviet officials.

The deal, now in the initial planning stage, would involve Western development of huge natural gas fields in the Yakutian region of East Siberia in return for deliveries of gas from the fields to Jpan and the West

Japanese-Soviet Accord
On Oil and Gas Is Signed

Japan was forced by America to renounce all wars and was not allowed to even have a standing army. Therefore Japan calls their rapidly growing army their Self-Defense Forces.

Renowned artist Helmut K. Wimmer paints his conception of the Black Hole in space. It remains a mystery.

"The good earth is not the only place in the universe where man can live. He probably can survive on at least one other planet in our solar system, and it looks more and more as if there are any number of planets in our galaxy with earthlike conditions — all man has to do is find them and get to them."

John P. Wiley, Jr.

Only time will verify whether Mr. Wiley's assumptions (on the left) are true or false. A little over 10 years ago scientists discovered the first celestial object (apart from the sun) known to emit X rays. A total of more than 120 X-ray sources have now been located and studied in detail. They include one neutron star, one quasar, two galaxies and a "black hole."

The black hole especially interests scientists. Some have suggested that it represents a large, burned out star which collapsed into something so dense that it became virtually invisible. Because of the collapsed star's enormous density, it is theorized, its gravity would be so strong that neither light nor any other form of radiation could escape from it. Even light or radiation passing close to it would be trapped.

Perhaps "speed" (velocity) holds the key to the "Black Hole in the sky." As we approach the speed of light, Einstein theorized, time slows down more and more. Very close to the speed of light, a *very small* increase can make a *drastic* change in the time period.

James W. Reid, who has done scientific research with the Space Division of General Electric, makes this interesting claim:

> If our astronauts
> could make a hypothetical trip to the near bright star Sirius (8.7 light years away) traveling at near the speed of light, it would take
> 2 months their time
> (18 months earth time).
> But if they could increase
> their speed by *less than* 5/100's of 1%
> they could fly to the nearest galaxy 2 million miles away
> (Andromeda) and back *in their lifetime*
> while earth aged *more than 3 million years!*

If this dramatic change occurs *near* the speed of light...what happens at the speed of light? In the ultimate, a person would live forever! *Aging would cease to occur at the speed of light*—At least that's the theory.

Physicists are now realizing that 90% of the Universe is nowhere to be seen. Signals are now known to be coming from an object in our galaxy that is many thousands of billions of miles from earth...with energy 1000 times more powerful than the sun. "The heavens declare the glory of God; and the firmament showeth His handiwork" (Psalm 19:1).

I PREDICT by 1982

It will become evident that life does exist somewhere else besides on the earth.
The mystery of flying saucers will be solved.

Giant Blasts in Milky Way 'Unprecedented'

Scientists Can't Fathom Mystery of Explosions at Galaxy's Edge

By JOEL N. SHURKIN

Inquirer Science Writer

A Canadian astronomer, playing with a 150-foot radio telescope, stumbled on an enormous, mysterious explosion near the edge of our galaxy "unprecedented" in the history of astronomy.

Three other blasts in the Milky Way were subsequently reported by astronomers.

All took place in the month of September. The frequency of the explosions and the nearness to our solar system were also unprecedented, astronomers say.

There appears to be no explanation for the source of the blasts. The first one sent the pen on the recorder "crashing off the scale," according to Dr. Philip C. Gregory, of the University of Toronto.

"Twenty seconds later the pen went back on the scale and crashed off again," he reported.

GREGORY and a team of astronomers were working the radio telescope at the Algonquin Radio Observatory, Ontario, Canada. They were studying the binary (double) star system of Algol.

During the period when Algol was below the horizon the astronomers used the time to study radio wave emissions from stars not known to be sources.

The waves from these stars are generally so weak it takes a half hour for the computer to gather enough information to form a pattern on a recorder.

On Sept. 2, Gregory had just aimed the telescope at Cygnus X-3, a weak source of X-ray waves in the constellation Cygnus (the Swan), an arm of the Milky Way. Normally a radio wave reading of one-half flux would be considered interesting, Gregory said. But whatever happened in that area suddenly blew the pen off the scale.

Later readings showed it hit 21 flux units, 1,000 times normal.

OTHER OBSERVATORIES were alerted and quickly confirmed the readings. French astronomers located it behind some dust clouds at the edge of the galaxy — closer than any explosions have ever been reported.

There are many sources of radio transmissions from deep space. It is believed they are clouds of electrons trapped in magnetic fields. Generally these are the result of gigantic explosions, some of them large enough to be the equivalent of the death of 100 million stars.

Because Gregory's explosion produced radio waves but not X-rays, some astronomers now doubt the September blasts came from Cygnus X-3.

THE CHANGING UNIVERSE

The illustration on the left shows the surface of the sun with its erupting storms.

Pictured below the sun are the planets shown in their relative size to the sun.

Reading from left to right they are:

1. MERCURY
   (closest to the sun)
2. VENUS
3. EARTH
4. MARS
5. JUPITER
6. SATURN
7. URANUS
8. NEPTUNE
9. PLUTO
   (furthest from the sun)

Jupiter has a diameter 11 times as large as the earth's. Mercury's diameter is less than half that of earth. It is interesting to note that all nine planets together weigh *less than a hundredth as much as the sun!*

Planets do not produce their own heat and light. Unlike stars, all light and nearly all heat on the planets comes to them from the sun.

While only 88 Earth-days make a year on Mercury...the length of a year on Pluto is 90,700 Earth-days!

In February, 1972 the United States launched the longest space mission in history. Its primary goal, to send back to earth some 2 years hence (by February 1974) close-up pictures of Jupiter. As "Pioneer 10" passes Jupiter, the gravity of the planet will seize it and whip it out of the solar system. It will sail indefinitely through the vast reaches of the Milky Way Galaxy, carrying a message in the form of a gold-coated aluminum plate. The message shows a man and a woman..."to let others know we are here."

Astronomers are becoming increasingly aware of strange, unexplainable occurrences in the universe. We do know that in the Tribulation Period there will be changes in the heavens (Revelation 8:8-12). Is the stage already being set?

163

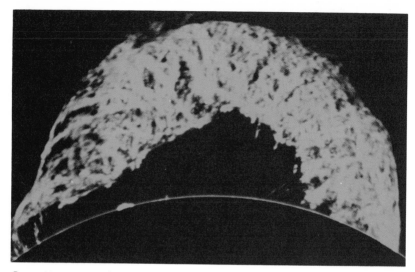

Some 16 unmanned spacecraft and instruments in orbit monitored the huge storm on the sun in August, 1972. Some startling information about the solar wind was uncovered.

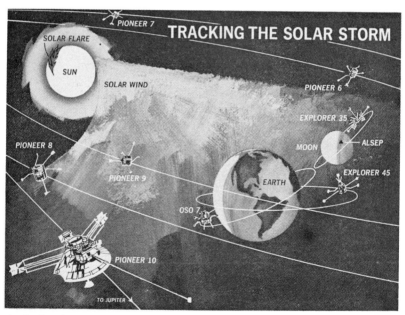

TRACKING THE SOLAR STORM

PIONEER 7
SOLAR FLARE
SUN
SOLAR WIND
PIONEER 6
EXPLORER 35
PIONEER 8
ALSEP
MOON
PIONEER 9
EXPLORER 45
EARTH
OSO 7
PIONEER 10
TO JUPITER

At the height of the solar storm on August 2, Pioneer 9 was 72 million miles from the sun. Its sensors clocked the storm-whipped solar wind racing past at 2.2 million miles per hour.

On August 7th alone solar physicists reported that the storm unleashed in **one hour** as much energy as the United States would consume in 100 million years!

THE MYSTERIES OF OUTER SPACE

Man, in reaching the moon, has **not even** touched the fringes of outer space!

I PREDICT by 1974

Scientists from around the world will converge in a special conference to determine what they believe is possible evidence that life does exist on other planets.

The Soviets have already revealed that they conducted two experiments last year designed to intercept signals from what they term "distant civilizations."

Many American and Soviet scientists appear to agree that other worlds have probably developed along lines very similar to those of the earth in its early history.

As Christians we are aware that there are 3 Heavens:

The Atmospheric Heavens

It is no higher than 20 miles above the earth.

The Celestial Heavens

This is the sphere in which the sun and moon and stars appear. (I Kings 8:27)

The Believer's Heaven

This is the abode of God and is characterized by holiness because God dwells there (John 14:2).

Man's search for life in outer space will result in dismal failure... although it will develop rockets and planes that can go at fantastic speeds.

I PREDICT by 1985 a hypersonic transport plane will be developed that flies 6000 miles an hour...going from Los Angeles to Australia in 1 1/2 hours.

IF YOU ARE A BELIEVER IN CHRIST, ONE DAY YOU WILL TAKE A TRIP INTO OUTER SPACE and meet the Saviour. No one knows the date for your trip. But we do know it is a certainty! (1 Thessalonians 4:13-18)

THREE HEAVENS

The word *heaven* is used hundreds of times in the Bible.
The primary meaning of *heaven* is "*that which is above.*"
In God's Word *heaven* refers to one of three major realms
as noted below.

THE HEAVENS	WHERE IS IT	SOME REFERENCES IN SCRIPTURE
THE ATMOSPHERIC HEAVENS	The atmosphere which surrounds the globe. Our troposphere is a blanket of air around earth. It is no higher than 20 miles above the earth. Most clouds are within 7 miles of the earth.	The Israelites were told that the land they were to possess "is a land of hills and valleys and drinketh water of the rain from heaven" (Deut. 11:11). See also Deut. 11:17, II Chron. 7:13, Isa. 55:9-11, Psalm 147:8, Matthew 24:30, Zach. 2:6.
THE CELESTIAL HEAVENS	This is the sphere in which the sun and moon and stars appear. I Kings 8:27 speaks of the Celestial Heavens when it says, "Behold, the heaven of heavens cannot contain God."	"And God said, Let there be lights in the firmament of the heaven to divide the day from the night..." (Genesis 1:14). "... Look now toward heaven, and tell the stars, if thou be able to number them..." (Genesis 15:5). See also Hebrews 1:10, Psalm 33:6, Isaiah 14:12, Amos 5:26 and Jeremiah 23:24.
THE BELIEVERS HEAVEN (The Abode of God)	This is characterized by holiness because God dwells there. Believers also will dwell in God's heaven because they have been made holy by the grace of God. Jesus assured us of the *reality* of this place (John 14:2).	"... I dwell in the high and holy place, with him also that is of a contrite and humble spirit..." (Isaiah 57:15). "Look down from heaven, and behold from the habitation of thy holiness and of thy glory..." (Isaiah 63:15). See also Exodus 20:22, Deut. 4:36, Matthew 3:17, Matthew 14:19, Acts 7:55 and John 3:27.

For a fuller treatment of this subject we recommend: THE BIBLICAL DOCTRINE OF HEAVEN, Wilbur M. Smith, Published by MOODY PRESS, Chicago, Illinois
Copyright © 1973 by Salem Kirban

THE RESURRECTIONS

Heaven

Resurrection of Christ and Ascension into Heaven

Acts 1:1-11
Matthew 27:50-53

(Matthew 27:52-53 tells of others who were resurrected after Christ—these were the wave-sheaf of the harvest to come. Leviticus 23:10-11.)

Paradise

Believers who have died before the Rapture. Present in a celestial, spiritual body.*

"And Jesus said unto him, Verily I say unto thee, Today shalt thou be with me in paradise."
Luke 23:43

"We are confident, I say, and willing rather to be absent from the body, and to be present with the Lord."
2 Corinthians 5:8

Believers meet with Christ in the air
1 Thessalonians 4:16

"...the dead in Christ shall rise First."
"Then we which are alive and remain shall be caught up together with them in the clouds to meet the Lord in the air....." 1 Thessalonians 4:16-17

Judgment Seat of Christ

"For we must all appear before the judgment seat of Christ....."
2 Corinthians 5:10
Believers now in New Bodies

Resurrection of Tribulation Saints
Daniel 12:1-2

Marriage of the Lamb
Revelation 19:7-9

Christ Returns to Earth with His Saints
1 Thessalonians 3:13, Zechariah 14:4

Great White Throne

"And whosoever was not found written in the Book of Life was cast into the Lake of Fire."
Revelation 20:15

Unbelievers cast into Lake of Fire eternally

Resurrection of the Dead Unbelievers
Revelation 20:11-13, Jude 6

"And I saw the dead, small and great, stand before God; and the books were opened; and another book was opened, which is the book of life: and the dead were judged out of those things which were written in the books, according to their works.
And the sea gave up the dead which were in it; and death and hell delivered up the dead which were in them: and they were judged every man according to their works."
Revelation 20:12-13

About A.D. 30	This Present Age	A.D.?	Rapture	Seven Year Tribulation Period	Mount of Olives Armageddon	1000 Year Millennial Age	With Satan Antichrist and False Prophet

*Physical body remains in grave awaiting Rapture

Stay Ready for Nuclear War, U.S. Told

U.S. Survey Puts World Outlay For Arms at $204-Billion Peak

By BENJAMIN WELLES
Special to The New York Times

WASHINGTON, May 5—The world's military spending—inflated by continuing price increases—reached a peak of about $204-billion last year, the United States Arms Control and Disarmament Agency said today.

In releasing its fifth annual survey of military spending and related data covering 1969-70, the agency said that this outlay was the equivalent in dollar terms of a year's income produced by the 1.8 billion people in the poorer half of the world's population.

However, it noted that in actual expenditure the increase in military spending over the previous year was the "smallest in

was a further rise in military budgets in 1970 prices, especially in "developing" countries.

It was also noted that more public funds continued to flow into military programs than into public education or public health programs.

In "developing" countries, for examples, the increase in military spending since represented, the agency "the equivalent of three expenditure on public tion for the billion sch children in those count

Other Highlight

Other points highli the report were the f In current prices, spending in the North

Two-Pronged Threat Exists, Moorer Says

WASHINGTON (UPI). — Adm. Thomas H. Moorer said Wednesday that the United States must stay strong enough to be prepared to fight a nuclear war with both the Soviet Union and China at the same time.

Moorer, chairman of the Joint Chiefs of Staff, said that was a necessity "regardless of how the relations among these three nations may develop in the future."

"Even if we were involved in a nuclear war with only one of these nations," Moorer said, "we would still need sufficient strategic forces to deter — simultaneously — a

ADM. THOMAS MOORER
. . . sounds warning

MORE SAFEGUARDS ON A-BOMBS URGED

Homemade Nuclear Devices Possible, Professor Says

By ANTHONY RIPLEY
Special to The New York Times

WASHINGTON, Nov. 14 — Control of nuclear material to prevent the building of homemade atom bombs by mentally disturbed people, ambitious small nations or by gangsters should be made a top-priority item, a University of Virginia law professor told the American Nuclear Society today.

"No doubt some old nations will break up and some new ones will appear; perhaps we are all doomed to the same disintegration that ended the Roman Empire . . ."

Ambassador
Charles W. Yost

"We have had our last chance. If we do not now devise some greater and more equitable system, Armageddon will be at our door."

General Douglas MacArthur

"The whole country is a mass grave. Who knows how many millions have been killed?"

General Abdul Khaliq
Describing the slaughter of East Pakistanis in 1971

The countries of the world seem now to be assembling into the final patterns that will lead to the world's finale at ARMAGEDDON. Armageddon, named for Mt. Megiddo, is the great Esdraelon-Jezreel Valley through the mountains of Israel. Here the final battle of the ages will be fought not too many miles from Jerusalem.

The Battle of Armageddon will be the Waterloo of all who oppose God. It will be a battle of the rulers of this earth against the King of Kings (Revelation 16:16).

The nuclear-arms race is spreading despite the superpower pacts... with at least 31 nations declining to sign the 1963 treaty. Even the big powers keep on testing new bombs—there have been 370 atomic explosions since the Treaty of 1963. A nuclear holocaust could kill over 100 million people in the U.S. alone.

Besides atomic weapons one researcher reports that a new laser-beam weapon is being developed that will make nuclear weapons and even modern armies obsolete. Arsenals of chemical and biological weapons are continuing to stockpile!

The four major blocs of power that will participate in the Battle of Armageddon are now, for the most part, already forming.

The United States of Europe
This bloc of nations has over 1.1 million combat troops and it is quite likely that a unified Europe, possibly combined with the United States, will become a reality in the not too distant future.

The Northern Confederacy
Russia has solidified her front and now has over 1.2 million combat troops in her arsenal of war.

The Asiatic Confederacy
Recognition of Red China by the UN, and the President's trip to Red China...have given China more prestige and consequently, more world leverage. These moves have also navigated Japan toward an alliance with China.

The Arab Confederacy
Daniel 11:40 seems to describe this world power. While not solidified at this time, we see evidences that the Arab bloc will soon unite.

At Armageddon, these 4 major blocs of nations will converge. The Lord Jesus Christ will come down from Heaven and wipe out the combined armies of more than 200 million men. The blood bath covers over 185 miles of Israel. Read in the New Testament, Revelation 14:20; 16:16; and 19:11-21.

I PREDICT by 1983

25 nations will have nuclear bombs.
There will be a stockpile of over 9000 nuclear bombs.
A nuclear bomb will be exploded in a warfare situation.

The Americans came to Vietnam and established several records. This was the United States' longest war, it was the farthest away from home. It had the most Presidents involved. It was the most we have ever outnumbered an enemy. The Paris peace talks began May 13, 1968 and final agreement was reached in early 1973.

It costs approximately $10,000 to kill an enemy soldier in World War 2. In the Vietnam War it has been estimated that the cost per kill is close to $500,000!

The Americans came to Vietnam. Now they are gone.

And the Asian sands are blowing over the footprints.

Battles of greater magnitude, however, are on their way. And the scene in the photograph to the right will be repeated over and over again. For man will not find peace. The whole world is engulfed in building up an arsenal of armament. It will lead to Armageddon.

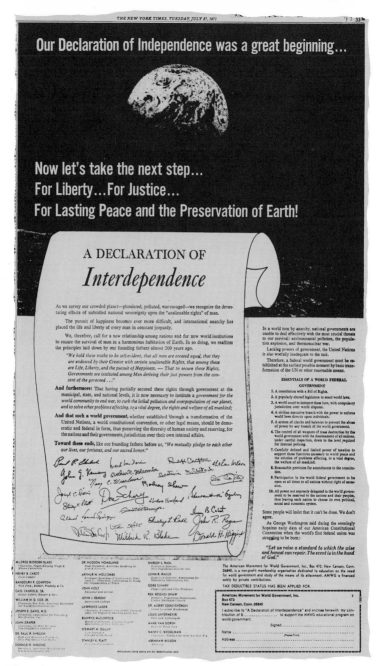

This ad appeared in The New York Times sponsored by The American Movement for World Government, Inc. urging that a world government be established "...at the earliest possible moment...."

THE MERRY MONTH OF MAY 1972

Take any month of the year and catalog the violence and tragedy. It may shock you. Buried in between hundreds of other news items... the blaring of the soap operas on TV...and man's dash to material gain...we sometimes fail to notice the world around is deteriorating. Take any month...take, May 1972, for instance:

MAY 1   Bomb blast in Northern Ireland textile plant.
1 killed. 15 injured.

MAY 2   Fire in Kellogg, Idaho silver mine.
91 killed.

MAY 5   Alitalia jet crashes in Italy.
115 killed.

MAY 7   Man goes beserk in East St. Louis, Illinois.
5 killed.

MAY 8   Arab guerillas hijack Belgian jetliner.
2 killed. 97 held hostage.

MAY 10   Mob tars and feathers 15-year-old girl in Belfast. Pulls her hair out by roots.

MAY 11   British cargo ship swept by fire near Uraguay.
83 die.

MAY 11   Five bombs explode in U.S. Army headquarters in Frankfurt, Germany.
1 killed. 13 injured.

MAY 14   Bomb explodes in car in Belfast. Students and police clash in Malagasy.
25 killed. 305 injured.

MAY 15   Governor Wallace makes a speech in Laurel, Maryland
3 injured.

MAY 17   Crowded commuter train struck in Brazil.
13 killed. 40 injured.

MAY 19   Two bombs explode in German publishing house.
17 injured.

MAY 22   Bomb explodes in car in Belfast parking lot.
60 injured.

MAY 24   Bombs go off in two cars in U.S. Army compound in Heidelberg, Germany.
3 killed. 5 injured.

MAY 29   Gunman sprays bullets into crowd at Raleigh, N.C.
4 killed. 8 injured.

MAY 30   Three Japanese open fire on travelers at Tel Aviv's Lod International Airport.
26 killed. 77 injured.

MAY 30   Memorial Day weekend traffic exodus.
565 killed. Thousands injured.

The year 1971. The place...Dacca. A handful of Mukti Bahini guerrillas of East Pakistan were conducting public executions by bayonet while 5000 Bengalese watched.

A young boy, recognizing one of the intended victims, rushed to the soldier to plead for his friend's life. He too was bayoneted and stomped to death. In this war, millions died.

The coming years will witness even greater inhuman tragedies. One day Christians will be persecuted...some will die a martyr's death. Israel's strange alliance with Antichrist will backfire and a reign of terror, such as she has never witnessed, will bring its toll of tragedy.

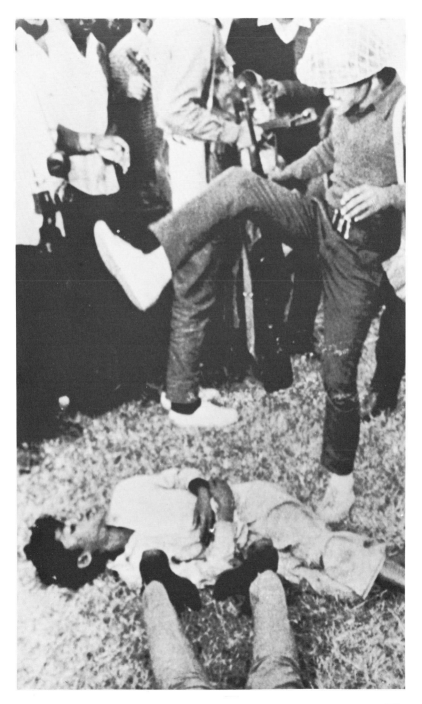

Not men from outer space but U.S. **soldiers rushed** to Washington, D.C. to quell disorders during a peace march on the Pentagon.

Is it difficult to imagine soldiers armed with sophisticated weaponry that instead of bullets fires a propellant of liquid or gas that will produce a sting like a scorpion...such as we read in the fifth trumpet judgment of Revelation 9:3-12?

THE FINAL ALIGNMENT OF NATIONS

At the end of Gentile world power, during the Tribulation Period, there will be three kingdoms and federations of nations who contest the authority of the **10 Federated States of Europe.**

1. The Northern confederacy

(Ezekiel 38:1-39:25 (esp. 38:15; 39:2); Daniel 11:40; Joel 2:1-27 (esp. 2:20); Isaiah 10:12; 30:31-33; 31:8-9)

You will find the principal passage describing this northern confederacy in Ezekiel 38:2-6.

Basically, here are the nations in the **northern** confederacy of Ezekiel 38:

A. Gog, Meshech, and Tubal (vs. 2) - Russia.
B. Persia (vs. 5) - Iran and Iraq.
C. Ethiopia and Libya (vs. 5) - Northeast Africa.
D. Gomer (vs. 6) - Germany (possibly East Germany).
E. Togarmah (vs. 6) - Exact location uncertain, but in the Europe, Turkey, Syria crescent.

2. The Asiatic confederacy

In Revelation 16:12 we read that Palestine, which will have become the center of the activity of Antichrist and his European federation...will be invaded by a great army coming from beyond the Euphrates known as the forces of "the kings of the east."

This is the second great alliance of powers that threatens the authority of the Federated States of Europe and Antichrist. The nations will most likely include: China, Japan, Vietnam, Thailand and other Asian countries.

3. The Arab confederacy

In Daniel 11:40 we find a third power in conflict with the European Federation of States. This is known as the King of the South. This power advances on Palestine and sets off a movement of nations that brings about its destruction. It would appear that the King of the South is Egypt aligned with other Arab nations and together allied with Russia (King of the North).

The above three alliances will challenge the ever growing power of Antichrist. Antichrist will be head of the 10 nation United States of EUROPE. This federation of states will probably include France, England, possibly West Germany and other Common Market countries and perhaps the Eastern European states now subservient to Russia. Perhaps even the United States will join this coalition of nations.

The prophecy is revealed in Revelation 17:12-13, which shows that these nations that were once a part of the Roman Empire will gather together and are going to enter into an agreement to give their authority to one man as their head (Daniel 7:7-8, 23-26 Cp. Revelation 13).

This one man will be the Antichrist!

Thus in the Tribulation Period we will find 4 great kingdoms as follows:

1. Russia and her allies (The Northern confederacy)
2. China and her allies (The Asiatic confederacy)
3. Egypt and her allies (The Arab confederacy)
4. United States of Europe (The 10 nation confederacy)

RUSSIA INVADES ISRAEL

The invasion of Palestine by Russia and her allies (The Northern confederacy) will bring Antichrist and his armies to the defense of Israel as her would-be protector.

Daniel 11:40-45 describes this invasion.

The following is a suggested order of events:

1. The campaign begins when Egypt and her allies (The Arab confederacy), move against the United States of Europe and Antichrist.

2. The Arab confederacy is joined by Russia and her allies (The Northern confederacy). Together they attack Antichrist's headquarters (Jerusalem) coming by land and sea.

3. Jerusalem is destroyed as a result of this attack (Zechariah 12:2). But the armies of The Northern confederacy are also destroyed (Ezekiel 39; Zechariah 12:4).

4. The full armies of Antichrist move into Palestine (Daniel 11:41) and conquer all that territory (Daniel 11:41-42). However Edom, Moab and Ammon will escape the tyrannical rule of Antichrist (Daniel 11:41). These areas are now in present day Jordan, and Petra is in the Edom section of Jordan.

Antichrist, under the great coalition of western nations (United States of Europe) will set up his headquarters in Jerusalem at the close of the Tribulation Period and reign over Israel. But not only will he reign over Israel and Europe but will also control the entire world.

China and her allies (The Asiatic confederacy) will march with 200 million men towards Jerusalem to contest the right of the United States of Europe to have world-wide dominion.

However, Antichrist, alarmed, decides to fight them on a battleground which will be to his advantage...the mountains of Judea (Mt. Megiddo).

When Antichrist with his western confederacy prepare to battle the Asiatic confederacy — suddenly the heavens open and the two opposing sides realize that some unusual occurrence is taking place directed by God. It is at this time they unite forces in order to devote all their energies into fighting the Lord Jesus Christ.

The battle at Armageddon is quickly over and Antichrist and the False Prophet are thrown into the Lake of Fire. The entire army is killed (Revelation 16:12-21; 19:11-21).

Antichrist, as leader of the United States of Europe, will set up his head-quarters in Jerusalem during the Tribulation Period. At the end of this 7 years China and her allies (The Asiatic confederacy) will march with 200 million men towards Jerusalem. China will contest the right of the United States of Europe to have world-wide dominion.

The Battle of Armageddon will ensue. Undoubtedly big guns will fire at each other across the plains of Esdraelon (Valley of Jezreel).

Suddenly the heavens open. The two opposing sides...witnessing this phenomena quickly turn their guns skyward...firing blindly at what will be perhaps the most startling sight of all history.

For what they will be firing at...find yourself a Bible and turn to the New Testament...the book of Revelation, chapter 19, verses 11-21. The results of this unusual conflict are found in verses 20 and 21.

The Plain of Esdraelon...ARMAGEDDON!

TRIBULATION and ARMAGEDDON
CASUALTY LIST

Below is a detailed list of casualties that will occur during the 7-year Tribulation Period including the Battle of Armageddon:

GENERAL CASUALTIES
AS A RESULT OF GOD'S JUDGMENT

"The Fourth Part of the Earth"	**Death** is due to the wars, famine and disease spread by the Four Horseman plagues of the Apocalypse (Revelation 6:1-8).
7000 in Jerusalem	**Death** is a result of an earthquake after Antichrist slays God's Two Witnesses (Revelation 11:13).
Mass Death	Worldwide earthquakes and giant hail cause **mass death** near the end of the Tribulation Period (Revelation 16:18-21).
Mass Death	**Mass death** occurs in the Antichrist's Capital City as it is suddenly destroyed by earthquake and fire (Revelation 16:19; cp. 18:5; all of chapter 18).
"Third Part of Men killed"	This third part of men are **slain** by the Army of 200 million. These appear to be the armies from the East, beyond the Euphrates. (Compare Revelation 9:14-16 with 16:12).
The Curia of the Apostate Church	These high religious officials are hunted down and **slain** by the followers of Antichrist, right after the middle of the Tribulation Period (Revelation 17:1,16,17).

THE MYSTERY CASUALTY

One Head of the Beast	Antichrist (and/or a geographical section of his empire) is **slain**...but by Satanic power lives again (Revelation 13:3)!

GOD'S MARTYRS SLAIN
by ANTICHRIST   (The Tribulation Saints)

Early Martyrs	Early martyrs are **slain** during the First Half of the Tribulation Period (Revelation 6:9-11).
God's Two Witnesses	The Two Witnesses of God are **slain** by Antichrist in the middle of the Tribulation Period... but God raises them up again after 3 1/2 days (Revelation 11:7,11,12)!
An Uncountable Number of Martyrs	Out of all nations, an uncountable number of martyrs is **slain** by Antichrist chiefly during the Second Half of the Tribulation Period, the "Great Tribulation" (Matthew 24:21-22; Revelation 7:9-17).

THE MARTYRED and SLAIN
OUT OF ISRAEL

Many of the 144,000

Many of the 144,000 believers chosen out of the Tribes of Israel will apparently be **slain** by Antichrist; and PERHAPS ALL OF THEM will be martyred. Thus in Revelation 14:1-5 these are seen already in heaven with Christ (Revelation 7:1-8).

Masses of Israelites

Masses of Israelites are **slain** by Antichrist in his Satanic attempt to destroy them so as to make it impossible for God to keep His promise to Abraham to give his seed the land of Israel. Zechariah 13:9 views "one-third" as the surviving remnant who are delivered by Christ (See also Zechariah 12:10). (Matthew 24:21; Daniel 12:1; Jeremiah 30:7; and Revelation chapter 12)

SLAIN by GOD at the
BATTLE OF ARMAGEDDON

Antichrist

The Antichrist is **cast alive directly into the Lake of Fire.** He is the Beast and the head of the Beast Empire (Revelation 19:19-21).

False Prophet

The False Prophet is **cast alive directly into the Lake of Fire** (Revelation 19:20).

The Massive World Armies and their Leaders

These massive world armies and their leaders who follow the Antichrist to Armageddon to destroy Israel are **all slain!** See Revelation 19:19-21.

The Massive Armies of the East

The Massive Armies of the East are **all slain.** They appear to be the 200 million of Revelation 9:14-16! Compare Revelation 9:14-16 with 16:12.

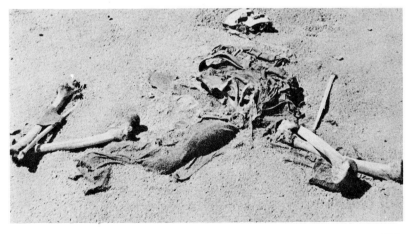

3 DECISIVE WARS

War	Participants	Occurs	Reason for War	Outcome	Scripture References
1	Russia and Allies (Arab nations, Iran, Germany) vs. Israel	Before or during first 3½ years of Tribulation Period (This could happen at any time!)	Russia desires Israel's vast mineral wealth.	God will intervene and through an earthquake in Israel plus rain and hail, the Russian army will be wiped out. It will take the Israelites 7 years to collect the debris. It will also take them 7 months to bury the dead!	Ezekiel 38:1-39:16
2 Battle of Armageddon	Armies from All Nations vs. God at Jerusalem	At End of 7 year Tribulation Period	Flushed with power Antichrist will defy God, seek to destroy the 144,000 witnessing Jews and Jerusalem.	The Lord Jesus Christ comes down from heaven and wipes out the combined armies of more than 200 million men. The blood bath covers over 185 miles of Israel and is "even unto the horse bridles." (Revelation 14:20) Antichrist and the False Prophet are cast alive into the Lake of Fire. (Revelation 19:20) Satan is bound in the bottomless pit for 1000 years. (Revelation 20:1-3)	Joel 3:9, 12 Zechariah 14:1-4 Revelation 16:13-16 Revelation 19:11-21 Ezekiel 39:17-29
3 The Final Rebellion	Satan vs. God	At End of 1000 year Millennium Period	God allows Satan one more opportunity on earth to preach his deceiving message.	Satan will be successful in deceiving vast multitudes (out of those born during the millennial period) to turn away from Christ. This horde of perhaps millions of people will completely circle the Believers in Jerusalem in a state of siege. When this occurs, God brings FIRE down from Heaven killing the millions in Satan's army. Satan is then cast into the Lake of Fire, where the False Prophet and Antichrist are, and they will be tormented day and night for ever and ever.	Revelation 20:7-10

THE Coming SEQUENCE of EVENTS in
God's Prophetic Timetable

As far as leading Bible believing scholars can understand the scriptures here are the future events **in the sequence they will occur** up to the Battle of Armageddon.

The **next** coming event on God's Timetable of prophecy is the **RAPTURE.** The word **Rapture** (to be "caught up") does not appear in the Bible. However it is used to describe the event of 1 Thessalonians 4:14-17 in which believers are "caught up" to be with Christ at His Second Coming.

In 1 Thessalonians 4:14-17 God's Word tells us:

> For the Lord Himself
> shall descend from Heaven with a shout...
> and the dead in Christ shall rise first:
> Then we which are alive and remain
> shall be caught up (RAPTURED)
> together with them in the clouds,
> to meet the Lord in the air:
> and so shall we ever be with the Lord.

RAPTURE refers to the time, prior to the start of the 7 year Tribulation Period, when believing Christians (both dead and alive) will "in the twinkling of an eye" rise up to meet Christ in the air.

Thus the SEQUENCE OF COMING EVENTS according to God's Word appears to be as follows:

RAPTURE including the FIRST RESURRECTION

(This can occur at any time.) At Christ's appearing the dead in Christ shall also rise (1 Thessalonians 4 and Revelation 20).

TRIBULATION

This will be a 7 year period, following the Rapture, of phenomenal world trial and suffering. It is at this time that Antichrist will reign over a federation of 10 nations which quite possibly can include the United States. See Daniel 9:27; Matthew 24:21.

JUDGMENT SEAT OF CHRIST

Here the believers raptured into heaven will stand before their Lord to receive crowns and rewards. Their sins have already been paid for at the cross (2 Corinthians 5:10).

BATTLE OF ARMAGEDDON

This will occur at the end of the 7 year Tribulation Period when the Lord Jesus Christ comes down from Heaven and wipes out the combined armies of more than 200 million men. The blood bath covers over 185 miles of Israel (See Revelation 14:20).

WHAT WILL YOU DO WITH JESUS?

After reading this book it should become evident to you that the world is **not** getting better and better.

We covered 20 reasons why. It would have been just as easy to list 100 reasons!

Never before in history have so many landmark events occurred so rapidly within so short a span of time. And each of these events are drawing us closer to the Rapture and then the 7 year period of Tribulation.

You will notice actual reproductions of news clippings on many of the pages. Brought together between the covers of this book... they have impact. Most people, however, glance at prophetic making headlines, then switch to the comic strips or Dear Abbey. And tomorrow's news is soon forgotten. But forgotten or not...each landmark news event brings us step upon step...one step closer to the holocaust of Armageddon!

I find it very easy to write books on the future and future events, analyzing the news in light of Bible prophecy. Why is it so easy? Because God so clearly outlined, in the Bible, events which are still to come. It's simply a matter of following the road map!

There are more than 300 Old and New Testament Scriptures which promise that Jesus Christ will return to earth! One verse in every 30 in the New Testament refers to Christ's Second Coming. There are 20 times as many references in the Old Testament to Christ's Second Coming as to His First Coming at Bethlehem!

And these promises will be fulfilled **just as literally** as the 200 Old Testament prophecies of His virgin birth, death, burial and resurrection were fulfilled in His first coming when He suffered and died for man's sins.

The important question is: **What will you do with Jesus?**

Will you simply say He was a good man who did good things?

Will you say His message is not relevant to our enlightened age?

Would you buy a car without first finding out the facts relevant to that car?

Would you invest money in a venture without first finding out details of that organization?

Would you get married without first finding out more about the individual with whom you pledge your entire life?

Your answer would probably be NO to each of these three questions.

Then WHAT ABOUT JESUS?
WHAT ABOUT HEAVEN?
WHAT ABOUT HELL?
WHAT ABOUT ETERNAL LIFE?
WHAT ABOUT ETERNAL DAMNATION?
WHAT ABOUT YOUR FUTURE AND THAT OF YOUR CHILDREN?

First, I am sure you will agree that your life here on earth will not go on and on. Any funeral director can attest to that fact. Any nurse or doctor can tell you that physical life on this earth someday ceases for each of us.

Second, if you have examined world conditions very carefully, you will admit that the world is certainly not getting better and better. Scientists even acknowledge the fact that the next 30 years will give us more complex problems in population growth, in famine, in crime, and in war.

Third, money (or the lack of it) will not cure your ills nor the ills of the world. Even if the wealth were spread out more evenly it would not resolve the problems. In actuality the spread of wealth worldwide on an even basis would make almost all Americans far poorer than they are now.

Fourth, if you look at it honestly, the permissive use of drugs and sexual freedom from the moral code will not build a better world.

Then what can you do?

Well, you can simply choose to ignore Christ and the Scriptures ...go on living your life, doing the best you know how to meet your problems, work and provide an income for your family, set aside a nest egg for retirement...

But THEN WHAT?

What happens when it comes time for you to depart from this earth?

Then WHAT WILL YOU DO WITH JESUS?

It takes NO DECISION on your part to go to Hell!

It does take a DECISION on your part, however, to go to Heaven!

> He that believeth on Him is not condemned:
> but he that believeth not is condemned already,
> because he hath not believed in the name of the
> only begotten Son of God. (John 3:18)

Here are five basic observations in the Bible of which you should be aware:

1. ALL SIN

> For all have sinned, and come short of the glory of God. (Romans 3:23)

2. ALL LOVED

> For God so loved the world, that He gave His only begotten Son, that whosoever believeth in Him should not perish, but have everlasting life (John 3:16)

3. ALL RAISED

> Marvel not at this: for the hour is coming, in which all that are in the graves shall hear his voice,

> And shall come forth; they that have done good, unto the resurrection of life; and they that have done evil, unto the resurrection of damnation. (John 5:28,29)

4. ALL JUDGED

> ...we shall all stand before the judgment seat of Christ. (Romans 14:10)

> And I saw the dead, small and great, stand before God; and the books were opened....(Revelation 20:12)

5. ALL BOW

> ...at the name of Jesus every knee should bow...(Philippians 2:10)

Right now, in simple faith, you can have the wonderful assurance of eternal life.

Ask yourself, honestly, the question....

WHAT WILL I DO WITH JESUS?

Will you accept Jesus Christ as your personal Saviour and Lord or will you reject Him?

This you must decide yourself. No one else can decide that for you. The basis of your decision should be made on God's Word—the Bible.

God tells us the following:

"...him that cometh to me I will in no wise cast out. (37)

Verily, verily (truly) I say unto you, He that believeth on me (Christ) *hath* everlasting life" (47)—(John 6:37, 47).

He also is a righteous God and a God of indignation to those who reject Him....

"...he that believeth not is condemned already, because he hath not believed in the name of the only begotten Son of God"—(John 3:18).

"And whosoever was not found written in the book of life was cast into the lake of fire"—(Revelation 20:15).

YOUR MOST IMPORTANT DECISION IN LIFE

Because sin entered the world and because God hates sin, God sent His Son Jesus Christ to die on the cross to pay the price for your sins and mine.

If you place your trust in Him, God will freely forgive you of your sins.

"For by grace are ye saved through faith; and that not of yourselves: it is the gift of God: (8)

Not of works, lest any man should boast" (9)—(Ephesians 2:8,9).

"...He that heareth my word, and believeth on Him that sent me, *hath* everlasting life, and shall not come into condemnation: but is passed from death unto life"—(John 5:24).

What about you? Have you accepted Christ as your personal Saviour?

Do you realize that right now you can know the reality of this new life in Christ Jesus. Right now you can dispel the doubt that is in your mind concerning your future and that of your loved ones. Right now you can ask Christ to come into your heart. And right now you can be assured of eternal life in heaven.

All of your riches here on earth—all of your financial security—all of your material wealth, your houses, your land will crumble into nothingness in a few years.

And as God has told us:

> "As it is appointed unto men once to die, but after this the judgment: (27)
>
> So Christ was once offered to bear the sins of many; and unto them that look for Him shall He appear the second time without sin unto salvation" (28)—(Hebrews 9:27, 28).

Are you willing to sacrifice an eternity with Christ in Heaven for a few years of questionable material gain that will lead to death and destruction? If you do not accept Christ as your personal Saviour, you have only yourself to blame for the consequences.

Or would you right now, as you are reading these very words of this book, like to know without a shadow of a doubt that you are on the road to Heaven—that death is not the end of life but actually the climactic beginning of the most wonderful existence that will ever be—a life with the Lord Jesus Christ and with your friends, your relatives, and your loved ones who have accepted Christ as their Saviour.

It's not a difficult thing to do. So many religions and so many people have tried to make the simple Gospel message of Christ complex. You can not work your way into heaven—*heaven is the gift of God to those who believe in Jesus Christ.*

No matter how great your works—no matter how kind you are—no matter how philanthropic you are—it means nothing in the sight of God, because in the sight of God, your riches are as filthy rags.

> "...all our righteousnesses are as filthy rags..." (Isaiah 64:6)

Christ expects you to come as you are, a sinner, recognizing your need of a Saviour, the Lord Jesus Christ.

Understanding this, why not bow your head right now and give this simple prayer of faith to the Lord.

Say it in your own words. It does not have to be a beautiful oratorical prayer—simply a prayer of humble contrition.

My Personal Decision for CHRIST

"Lord Jesus, I know that I'm a sinner and that I cannot save myself by good works. I believe that you died for me and that you shed your blood for my sins. I believe that you rose again from the dead. And now I am receiving you as my personal Saviour, my Lord, my only hope of salvation. I know that I'm a sinner and deserve to go to Hell. I know that I cannot save myself. Lord, be merciful to me, a sinner, and save me according to the promise of Your Word. I want Christ to come into my heart now to be my Saviour, Lord and Master."

Signed. . . . .

Date . . . .

If you have signed the above, having just taken Christ as your personal Saviour and Lord...I would like to rejoice with you in your new found faith.

Write to me...Salem Kirban, Kent Road, Huntingdon Valley, Penna. 19006...and I'll send you a little booklet to help you start living your new life in Christ.